CONTROL
ALL FEAR

A collection of true accounts of dangerous police
work and the process the author used to control fear
and cope with critical incident stress

MICHAEL C DYSON

Book #1 in the Peacemaker series

ACKNOWLEDGEMENTS

Dr. Roger Solomon, the Director at Critical Incident Recovery Resources, Arlington, Virginia is my inspiration for this book. My life changed when I met him and saw his model describing the dynamics of fear. In the best way I know how, I have endeavored to demonstrate and explain how his work has made my life so much safer and easier to cope with.

PREFACE

I am afraid of everything. Fear of being alone, fear of being hurt, fear of being made a fool of, fear of failure.... Still, I think all my fears stem from one big one.

—Tiffanie DeBartalo

Just one year after graduating from the Police Academy, I was nineteen years old, a Constable in the Tasmania Police Force, and I was terrified. Two men, one armed with a high-powered rifle, lay hidden in the long grass beside the highway. They had fired shots into a nearby house. This was the first time I had had to respond to an active shooter situation.

I had not been trained to deal with an active shooter, especially one with a high-powered rifle. I did not know where the two suspects were, but they were close, I was unarmed, and out in the open.

My oath of office was fresh in my mind. That oath meant everything to me then and it still does. I had to go out in the open, unarmed, and arrest the men. Taking no action would be neglect of my duty *and* an act of cowardice. Worst of all, I would break my sworn oath. Doing nothing was not an option.

With quaking knees and a shrinking gut, I took my first step into the most dangerous situation I had experienced in what I thought could be a short life.

You are going to read about what made me passionate about being able to deal with aggression and violence from that day on. To be a capable police officer, I realized that I must take control of fear. Fear of injury, death, incompetence, failure, mistake, punishment, and being made to look a fool were just a few of my early fears.

For the first ten years, experience and plain good luck got me through some sticky situations. Try as I might, I could not find any available training or reference material to fill the knowledge gap that I had about policing and law enforcement in life threatening situations.

Things started to change for me in 1985 when I bought a book on street survival during work experience in the USA. The book gave me broad insight and new ideas about dealing with violent people. I started to keep anything and everything I could find about fear, stress, aggression, and violence.

Over the years, I have adapted and used many processes for coping with different threatening circumstances. I created or adapted processes that were easy to remember in times of stress. They are designed to eliminate confusion and enable me to focus on what is important regardless of the chaos around me. I have used them on countless occasions in law enforcement, business, sport, and for personal challenges.

The process for coping with fear is one of those and it has never failed me. Tested me, yes, but failed me, no.

With growing experience, I discovered that many of the methods I used in life-threatening situations also applied to everyday life. I realized that other people could benefit from these methods in their daily lives too. Now I am ready to share them with the world in hope that many will be able to improve their lives by using them themselves.

MESSAGE FROM THE AUTHOR

One thorn of experience is worth a wilderness of warning

– William Shakespeare

Welcome to Control all Fears.

Have you ever wondered where people who work in dangerous occupations find the courage to do their jobs? I certainly have.

I joined Tasmania Police as a 16-year-old. I did not give a moment's thought to the danger involved in the job, and no one gave me any warning about what those dangers could be.

I naively joined 'the job' to protect and serve. Soon after graduating from the Academy, I quickly found myself experiencing almost overwhelming fear for my safety.

For the first 10 years, I was troubled by my fear of danger, especially when dealing with violent people. I searched for a way to get rid of my fear, but I could not find it.

I went through a stupid period of denial and reckless courage. I charged headfirst into danger with the hope that everything would work out. I survived that period through sheer luck.

By 1985 I was convinced that there had to be a way to prepare myself for danger. I asked men who had gone through dangerous situations how they did it. Invariably, their answer was always the same, "I knew what I was doing." It seemed that experience was the key to coping, but I worried that getting experience would get me hurt or killed if I did not know what I was doing.

Reading as much as I could find on police survival and street tactics helped me in the early days. The types of situations I might have to deal with were explained, and I imagined how I would deal with them. I set about learning and practicing the skills that I would need. Some people I worked with thought I was crazy and unrealistic.

The types of danger I envisaged were not going to happen in Tasmania, according to them.

Personal vindication came to me in 1988 when I met Dr. Roger Solomon. He is the Director at Critical Incident Recovery Resources, Arlington, Virginia. Dr. Solomon was a presenter at the first Critical Incident Stress Debriefing conference in Melbourne, Victoria.

Dr. Solomon's model for *Coping with Fear* showed me why thinking ahead, imagining scenarios, and training for them was not crazy. I am sure that using his model helped me avoid suffering from PTSD and come to understand myself so much better.

Anticipating and training for dangerous events helped me develop training programs and departmental policies and procedures for dealing with major incidents. All the events I predicted and prepared for eventuated in Tasmania, except for one – a significant bombing.

Many of my colleagues ignored the warnings of danger, preferring to believe that the scenarios I talked about would never happen in Tasmania. Sometimes I felt that the scenarios I developed for training courses were not taken seriously enough by other instructors or the participants.

People who deny or ignore potential danger often react poorly when the shock of it happening hits them. Practical and realistic thinking is lost. Panic, uncertainty, and fear overwhelm people.

The most courageous people I have met were those who were not taken by surprise. They were the type of people who knew, 'it was bound to happen one day.' These were great decision-makers and great leaders in times of chaos.

The greatest cowardice and worst coping I witnessed was in people who ignored the reality of a situation and were unable to think clearly because they were shocked and paralyzed by fear.

It is not only police officers I am referring to. I am including victims of accidents, crime, and disasters, family crisis, personal threats, mass casualty incidents, families, friends, and communities. The first dominant emotion that can overwhelm people is fear.

Often, the first thing a police officer must deal with in a crisis is fear, either his own or someone else's, often both. Rational and effective responses to a crisis depend on fear being brought under control.

The approach I follow has given me confidence in my ability to stay safe and overcome all the challenges, obstacles, and crises I have faced.

I believe in it so strongly that I want to share it with everyone who wants to learn how to cope with any fear they have.

WHY I WROTE THIS BOOK

"I don't regret anything I've ever done in life, any choice that I've made. But I am consumed with regret for the things I did not do, the choices I did not make, the things I did not say. We spend so much time being afraid of failure, afraid of rejection. But regret is the thing we should fear most. Failure is an answer. Rejection is an answer. Regret is an eternal question you will never have the answer to. "What if..." "If only..." "I wonder what would have..." You will never, never know, and it will haunt you for the rest of your days."

— Trevor Noah, Born a Crime: Stories from a South African Childhood

When I started working in the Tasmania Police Force in 1974 there was no information like today to help you understand fear and how it affects your ability to think. We were expected to face up to whatever came our way and just get the job done.

The training we received was harsh by today's standards and mentoring by senior officers could be brutally honest. However, I would not have it any other way. I suspect that a lot of the stress related problems in policing these days are because the selection and training of officers is not preparing them properly for the job.

I have delivered lectures to hundreds of people in a wide range of occupations on dealing with occupational aggression and violence. I have investigated many threats against individuals and corporates. The most common obstacle to convincing people that aggression could be managed, and violence can be prevented was the fear they expressed. People appeared to understand that it could be done, but not by them. Fear held them back.

In writing this book, I reveal what I have done to overcome fear in the hope that others can use the same process to overcome any fears they have.

I explain how to move beyond being afraid of anything and how to avoid harmful negative thoughts after experiencing a critical incident. I will explain the process that I have used for decades to enable me to find courage to act and to cope with the stress of multiple critical incidents.

Truly, this process has helped me cope with all my fears ranging from my fear of heights all the way through to dealing with violent people, even including dealing with the death threats I still receive occasionally. I believe it will help you too.

I believe that everyone should learn how to accept fear, how to minimize the fear factor when facing danger, and how to eliminate confusion as an incident develops. You can learn how to know your true capability and capacity to respond in threatening situations, and how to choose your best response. Do this and peace of mind follows.

WHO IS THIS BOOK FOR?

Do not believe you are weak. All power is within you. By understanding the situation, you can cope with anything and do everything necessary to succeed.

This book is for those who face situations that make them afraid and unsure of how to move forward to victory over whatever that situation may be.

There comes a time when most of us face a mountain that seems too hard to climb – we can get stuck in a valley of fear, anxiety, and stress. Our trouble seems overwhelming, and a pathway over or around our mountain is often out of sight.

What are you afraid of? What you read on the internet, snakes, the dark, heights, deep water, rejection, love, spiders, moths, the unknown, public speaking, flying, storms, failure, death, dishonor? Everyone is afraid of something. Or are they?

What about people who never seem to be afraid? Why are there people, especially young people, who are completely unafraid of taking risks and then others who seem afraid of everything? Why are some people able to perform amazing feats of courage that others would never contemplate doing? What about soldiers and police officers who confront life threatening danger as part of their job? How do they do it?

Fear's purpose is to keep us from harm, but what if it holds us back from what we really want? What if fear stops us from doing something that we have to do for the sake of ourselves, family, or our jobs?

What causes fear in the first place? Is our fear triggered by something that is dangerous or something we simply think is dangerous? What about being around other people who are afraid? Can we become afraid simply because people around us are afraid?

What makes people courageous in the face of danger? How do they become brave enough to face danger and risk? What if we give in to fear and avoid doing what we must do, or what we would enjoy doing? What effect will that have on our self-respect and inner peace of mind?

Is it wise to simply push ourselves to face extremes without knowing what we are getting ourselves into? Should we just ignore fear and push ahead as though it was not there? Can bravado help us survive dangerous situations?

These are all questions that I had to find answers for, not only for day to day living but especially for my career in law enforcement. It has taken me over 30 years of reading, research, and personal experience to come up with answers. Using everything I have learned and experienced, I have come up with a simple approach that anyone can use to overcome fear and find the courage to face adversity.

No matter your age, you will never overcome a fear holding you back by walking away from it. If you follow the approach I explain in this book, you will find courage by being able to focus on what you need to do to cope with any fear that comes your way.

I have written this book to shed light on a pathway that can get you through difficult times and bad experiences.

Having the ability to control all fear will increase your self-respect and give you peace of mind. You will be able to make wise decisions when fear tries to overwhelm you. You will also find that this ability will decrease stress and anxiety caused by experiencing fear.

Are you in a violent and abusive relationship, always afraid? Do you work in a risky and dangerous job? Are you fearful that the world has become a more dangerous place?

These are just a few types of situations that create great fear and make people feel helpless and vulnerable.

Everyone experiences fear that has the potential to freeze up or react in harmful ways.

Fear can be real or imagined and we all need a way to work out which is which. We need to be able to overcome real and imagined fear to be able to rapidly make the best decision to keep us safe from harm.

It is said that when you ignore your fear, it grows. When you face your fear, it shrinks. I found this to be true, but it took me years of study and practice to work out the best way to face fear.

Do you want to master your emotions and face your fears? Do you want more control over adversity or danger? Do you want help on how to replace anxiety with confidence? If you answer yes to any of those questions, this book will set you on the right path.

HOW IS THIS BOOK STRUCTURED?

To make the book easier to read and the information easier to follow, I have divided it into three main parts.

The first part is the backstory. These are stories of things that happened to me without warning during a typical day's work. There is nothing heroic or special in them. They will show that bad things happened to make me feel fear, sorrow, shock, surprise, vulnerability, and lastly, awareness. Repeatedly experiencing those feelings drove me to find a way to cope with fear and find the courage to handle the stuff I did not like.

I hope the stories create a picture of why I became so interested in the subject of fear and dealing with angry and aggressive people. They are not the most dramatic or dangerous examples of situations I have experienced, however. I believe they adequately set the context to help explain my process to control fear later in the book.

The second part of the book contains some helpful information to understand fear, how to make wise decisions in times of crisis, and coping with stress. It is not possible to cover everything you should or could know on this subject, but this is the information that I found to be most helpful to me.

By the time you reached that part of the book, I hope you will see how important it is for everyone to be able to cope with fear. We need to be able to face our fears. At best, fear will hold us back. At worst, it can cause debilitating mental and physical health problems.

The third and final part is the most important. It is where I explain the dynamics of fear and how to take a fast track to a rapid response to danger. I explain the five steps that anyone can take to overcome fear.

Follow these five steps and you will be the person leaving others standing in your wake with jaws hanging slack as you explode into action. You will become a victor over fear holding you back, not a victim of it.

Whether it is cyber-bullying, workplace, family, or street violence, there is a way to respond to all of it, but the first step is to control your fear.

I hope you find the book entertaining, enlightening, and helpful.

TABLE OF CONTENTS

PART ONE –
A PIECE OF
HELL BREAKS
LOOSE

I am not concerned about all hell breaking loose, but that a PART of hell will break loose… it'll be much harder to detect.

— George Carlin

INTRODUCTION

Michael had a unique career that is unlikely ever to be repeated

– Luppo Prins, Assistant Commissioner of Police, 1997

Life's surprises come in all types, shapes, and sizes. They can be good, bad or downright ugly, and a day in the life of a cop can throw all of them in your face at any moment. I have selected these stories to help explain my journey to cope with fear. But first, here is a summary of my career in Tasmania Police.

According to my diaries, in my 25-year police career, I made 442 arrests, dealt with 91 violent offenders, of which 11 were armed.

My investigation experience included 13 murders and 52 serious sex crimes.

I received 5 genuine death threats, one of which was a planned assassination that was foiled thanks to an informant who refused to take part in the killing.

I attended 21 sudden deaths and investigated 15 suicides and negotiated 5 people out of committing suicide.

I was the youngest officer officially appointed as "Detective" at the age of nineteen. I started working as a detective in the Burnie Drug Squad with the longest-serving detective in the history of Tasmania Police, Fred Harris. Neither of those records is likely to be broken.

The first 6 months of 1976 were spent walking the beat in Hobart. Just like every other Constable, I cut my teeth on drunk and disorderly, assaults, vagrants, and other street crimes.

I transferred to Burnie Uniform Branch mid- 1976. I worked in general uniform duties roles like staffing the inquiry office and radio room, walking the beat, and general patrol car duties. I spent 14 ½ months relieving in the Drug Bureau in Burnie, where I was appointed as a Detective after a short probationary period.

In December 1979, I transferred to the Burnie Criminal Investigation Branch where I was very fortunate to be trained and mentored by experienced criminal investigators.

I transferred to the Devonport Criminal Investigation Branch in June 1983 where I was partnered with a very experienced Detective Sergeant. Our investigation into the attempted murder of Sir Reginald Wright was ground breaking in several areas.

In April 1985, I was promoted to Detective Senior Constable and transferred to the George Town Criminal Investigation Branch. I was promoted to Detective Sergeant there in August 1987.

The George Town Criminal Investigation Branch covered the largest geographical area in Tasmania. The type of crime we investigated was as varied as you could imagine. I even arrested two illegal immigrants there!

I was asked to join the Tasmania Police Special Operations Group in 1987. I had never considered it before but jumped at the chance. Known as the SOG, the group was trained to combat terrorism and dangerous armed criminals. I believed that the specialized training they received would help me develop knowledge and skills to deal with violent criminals.

In March 1989, I transferred to the Bellerive Criminal Investigation Branch for a short time before moving to the Hobart CIB in May 1989. I worked in the major crime team, fraud squad, child protection unit, violent crime squad, general squad, arson unit, and gaming sections.

I was promoted to Detective Senior Sergeant but spent most of my time relieving as an Acting Inspector.

I am probably the only Detective Senior Sergeant that held four higher-duty positions at the same time. For one week I was Course Director on a Crisis Command course, OIC Protective Security, OIC Forensic Division, and OIC Community Relations Bureau.

Between 1992 and 1994, I was the Second in Charge of the Crime and Drugs Liaison division within Operations Support. I was the single full-time Special Operations Group officer responsible for organizing training, developing tactic responses, departmental policy and procedures for violent incident management, and planning special operations activities.

In 1994, I was asked to relieve the Inspector at the Community Relations Bureau. Initially, I objected, saying, "I'll be going from ass-kicking to baby kissing." It was told that it was a career move, so I spent a year overseeing crime prevention programs. This was when I designed and implemented the Bush Watch crime prevention program.

I was moved out of the position because one of the Commissioners' staff officers wanted my job to build his CV. I objected to the move because he thought he had applied for the senior position, but I held the senior position.

Not surprisingly, given the systemic corruption in Tasmania Police at the time, a new position was created for me as Second in Charge of the Protective Security Section.

I moved into the Protective Security Section in 1995. I remained there until I resigned from Tasmania Police on the 22nd of August 1997. At that time, I was the State Firearms Training Coordinator, Special Operations Group Training Cell and Assault Teams Commander, and Counter-terrorist coordinator and exercise writer. This was one of the most stressful times in my career, working across many areas, making changes in policy and procedures, and leading people through changes in the way we operated.

In 1997 I formed a private investigation and security business. At one time, my company employed over 180 people and held all the major State government security contracts. However, I was the victim of two significant bad debts, one in 2000 and another in 2008. The last one, almost $250,000, led to my business's liquidation in 2011, when it was valued between $1.8 and $2.4 million.

I now work as a law enforcement consultant on forest law enforcement and the illegal wildlife trade in South East Asia. I have also worked in Armenia on forest law enforcement and governance, and more recently, in the South Pacific Communities.

I received numerous commendations during my police service and have received the following honors: Australian National Medal; National Police Service Medal; Tasmania Police Service Medal; and the Australian Security Medal.

Almost twenty-five years of dealing with death, danger, violence, crisis, chaos were bad enough. Add to that the internal challenges and threats: workplace bullying, systemic corruption, manipulation, harassment, and threats to job security created a permanent vulnerability state.

The trouble with the internal threats was that you did not always know the source of the danger. Some officers made the bullets, and others fired them. Back-stabbing was an art form.

The last three years of my police career were a life of stress, anger, and abject hatred for a couple of individuals. The pressure came from trying to stay one step ahead of internal politics and avoiding trouble.

The anger came from the constant feeling of being used, abused, and under attack from senior officers. The hatred stemmed from the untouchable bosses who bullied so many good men out of the job, of which I was finally one.

My response to all the injustices I felt that I had suffered was to resign from the Police Force. It was the hardest decision of my life. Part of the decision was a resonant 'fuck you," and part of it was to run away from my anger issues that had developed to a dangerous level.

The good news is that developing the five steps to cope with fear helped me get rid of my anger and carry no lasting stress problems.

I have never looked back and I am lucky to still work in law enforcement.

BASTARDIZATION AND BULLYING

Don't let the bastards get you down.

— Margaret Atwood

"Gentlemen, this is not going to be an easy job," said Senior Sergeant Bernie McCann, Officer in Charge, Cadet Course 4/74.

It was early in January 1974, and I was irrigating a potato paddock on the farm when I received the news. Dad drove into the paddock, waving an envelope out of the Landrover window. I had an interview to join Tasmania Police.

After passing the interview and medical examination, my application to join the Tasmania Police was accepted.

I reported for duty on the 24th of February 1974, having just turned 16 years of age. I was the second youngest in my course.

There were 32 young men in Course 4/74. We were aged between 16 and 18 years of age, most of us were 16, and I think there were a couple of 17-year-olds and one 18. We lived and worked together for two years and became a brotherhood of men in ways that people would not understand unless they have experienced it.

There are so many great stories to tell about those two years of police training, which need to be told because they describe how we were trained and prepared for work on the streets.

We were made ready for police work in a totally different way from the police training methods of today.

The first morning, after the official opening of the course, we fell into our instructors' hands. They were Senior Sergeant Bernie McCann, Senior Constable "Chook" O'Rourke, PT instructor First Class Constable Graham Pedder, and drill instructor Sergeant Peter Connell.

How naïve I was!

I did not expect a policeman to swear, and it was then that I heard the word 'fuck' used as a punctuation mark. I sat through that first morning with my eyes bugged open and jaw hanging slack. It was a no holes barred introduction to policing.

Bernie McCann was a soft-spoken, hard-arse country cop. One of the first things I remember him saying is, "Gentlemen, this is not going to be an easy job."

He described the gory details of how people died and what we were expected to do with the deceased. He explained that we would often be working alone and would have to deal with the best and worst of human nature. He described what it was like to be first on the scenes of murder, suicide, car accidents, and other forms of sudden death.

He described what it was like to attend a pub brawl. He said that when turning up, "you work out who is the toughest and loudest person involved, and then you knock him out." he said. "That way, you will get everyone's attention and respect." By the way – that is still the best strategy.

He said the instructors would not only teach us the law and police procedures; they would lead us to be men. We were to become men who would be loyal to the badge and loyal to each other above all else. He said we would be fed well and given physical training to make us strong enough to stand up to the violence and other rigors of policing.

Self-discipline was forced on us, and it started with being confined to barracks for the first two weeks with no days off work. Every night was a study night; a high standard of academic achievement was expected.

It is fair to say that these three officers were my first experience with 'good cop, bad cop.' Bernie McCann was the elder statesman and clearly the boss. John O'Rourke and Graham Pedder were the good guys, and then there was Peter Connell.

Connell was a self-professed retired British Grenadier Guard. He wore his police cap with the brim cut down like a German SS officer, and he liked nothing better than to chew out and abuse the members of course 4/74.

He is the reason that Course 4/74 was blamed for the *Bastardization Inquiry* that took place in 1975.

By today's standards, Connell's oppressive behavior was appalling, but it was not so bad back then. However, one of our members was related to a senior officer. Over dinner one night, he revealed some of Connell's bully-boy tactics to him. The Inspector reported what he had been told to the senior command.

The subsequent "bastardization inquiry" resulted in transfers of some officers, including Connell, and Course 4 would be forever tarnished with the reputation for 'dobbing in' the instructors. It was the first, but not the last, internal investigation I was involved in.

One of Connell's mates was the driving instructor, Senior Constable Webb. For years after, he would call me Dobber Dyson. Dobber is a derogatory term like being called a narc or informer.

He knew I hated the insult, and it pissed me off every time he called me 'Dobber Dyson.' I never did anything about it and laughed it off.

The worst thing Webb did to me was to fail me on my first attempt at qualifying for my police driving permit.

I had been driving for several years, having learned to drive tractors and four-wheel drives on the farm, so there was no problem with my ability to drive. Webb failed me because I did not pull into the right-hand lane of Argyle Street three bloody blocks away from where I was to park on the right side of the road outside the Academy building! That was an act of bastardization.

Connell's antics did not hurt us one bit, and even after all these years, many of us admit that he helped make men out of us.

Indeed, the bastardization helped prepare me for coping with the workplace bullying that plagued the last years of my police career and ultimately led to my early retirement.

Here are a couple of examples of workplace bullying, the 1974 style.

We did marching drills, twice a week, at the Anglesea Army Barracks parade ground in Hobart. There was a flagpole at one end of the parade ground that Connell sent us to march to when we messed up a drill. His language was too florid to print here, but I think you will get the picture if I write it this way. When we made a mistake, Connell would put his hat brim up against our forehead (or close enough to it). He would pour out a mouthful of foul abuse, calling us whatever name came to his tongue and ordered the victim to repeat it. For example:

"Cadet Dyson, what are you!?"

"I am a police cadet, Sir!"

"You are NOT a police cadet; you are a dozy, snot-nosed cunt; now, what are you!?"

"I am a dozy, snot-nosed cunt, Sir!"

"Very good! Now we all know what you are, march over to that flagpole, and at the top of your voice, tell the flagpole what you are until I call you back!"

Playing games with him did not work out too well for us, although some of us tried. We would still be sent to the flagpole to repeat what he called us in our loudest voice.

It was funny to all but the victim at the time, and I reckon most of us got the opportunity to talk to the flagpole at one time or another.

I recall him catching me out on one occasion, muttering something abusive about him under my breath. I can remember the stink of his tobacco breath as he demanded that I repeat what I had said. I might have said something like, "one day I am going to knock you on your arse," because he said, "When you are old enough and tough enough, I will be in a fucking wheelchair, boy."

Every morning before work, the duty instructor conducted 'stand by your bed' room- inspections. We had to make our beds according to military standards with the sheets and blankets folded to an exact shape, size, and order. The bed cover had to be tucked in so tight that a coin would bounce when dropped onto the bed. Clothing had to be neatly folded in drawers or hung in wardrobes. Our room kept spotlessly clean in inspection order until the end of the day.

While we stood to attention at the end of the bed, Connell would inspect every nook and cranny with a white glove. Our evening or weekend leave was canceled if he found any dust. There is no way that sort of bastardization would be tolerated today.

Back in those days, people were selected for police service more by their backgrounds than their academic qualifications, which were mid-level qualifications as a minimum. I recall that the police cadet system was not popular among long-serving officers because eighteen was too young for the job. However, the training we received was robust, and cadets that lasted two years were reasonably seasoned by the time they graduated.

We weren't angels either!

Neville was not very fresh with his hygiene, so a mob of us ambushed him one night and gave him a bash-broom bath in cold water with all sorts of detergents and stuff in the water.

We all got fronted to the Inspector, but nothing much came of it. Neville turned up to a reunion a few years ago for the first time after resigning from the Force soon after graduation. It was great to see him and it gave me a chance to apologize to him for me being an arsehole.

As I said before, I have done many things that I am ashamed of, and one of those was to make fun of Ken's religious beliefs in front of the whole course. I am fairly sure I have apologized to Ken for that. I was a total arsehole then too.

Tojo was a Hobart city boy with a lot of street smarts. We celebrated his 17th birthday at his parents' house in Sandy Bay. I made a bet with the boys that I could scull a 10-ounce glass of Johnny Walker whiskey. I won the bet and made some money out of it, but it was not worth it.

I got crying drunk and remembered spewing over the back fence. Brett found me leaning on the wall outside the house, and I remember him laughing and kicking the legs out from under me, making fun of me.

I suffered that week during search and rescue training. I suffered from the hang-over and the shame of being a crying drunk. It took me years to be able to drink whiskey after that little episode.

In our first year in the Academy, we lived in a 2-story hostel in New Town called Woodlands. Someone got interested in Ouija boards, and out of that came one of the best pranks we ever carried out.

We set it up to have Tojo sit in on a session, and we created the message to him that he was to die at 11 pm that night.

Well, Tojo was shitting himself and wanted fellas to sit up with him all night, but of course, none did. We all went to bed, or so it seemed to Tojo.

Tojo had one of the few single rooms downstairs, and I snuck into it with a table tennis bat and climbed on top of his wardrobe, which was behind the door. Tojo carefully opened the door and shone a torch around to make sure it was safe to enter before he turned on the light. Just as he turned on the light, I threw the table tennis bat at his feet, making a hell of a racket on the wooden floor, and at the same time let out the best blood-curdling scream I could make.

His reaction was all that we hoped for. He let out a blood-curdling scream of sheer terror and almost jumped out of his skin before collapsing in a heap on the floor.

Naturally, course members found their place in the pecking order in the first year in the Academy. The instructors kept a tight reign on us, but at the same time, they allowed us to toughen each other up with a bit of mischief, skylarking and even bullying.

Bastardization and bullying are harmful behaviors. Not being afraid is the first step to protecting yourself from them, and we all toughened up during those two years. However, I didn't realize how much worse it would be outside the Academy.

TOUGH TRAINING

Preparation for law enforcement work requires hard work and harder discipline.

The military-style of discipline and training in 1974 was far different from the soft style used today. Physical skills training and study were relentless. It was physical, psychological, and intellectual, all rolled together.

On the days we weren't marching, we were doing physical training (PT) or occasionally playing sport. The first year was naval-style PT, but in the second year, we were given self-defense training by the newly hired Japanese judo champion, Taka Nakajima.

Taka was the original full-time physical training instructor employed by Tasmania Police, and he taught us judo and aikido.

We had to qualify with the Royal Life Saving Bronze Medallion before graduating, so swimming and life-saving training was a regular weekly activity.

Three 'education officers' provided weekly lectures and examinations in mathematics, English, social studies, psychology, and public speaking. The Police Chaplain lectured on religion & morals. We also had to qualify with first-aid certificates, and St. Johns Ambulance supplied that training.

An external trainer provided instruction in touch typing. All of us had to achieve 25 words per minute, with 90% accuracy by the end of the course.

Police Academy instructors provided most of the lectures on Police Regulations & Standing Orders, practical police duties. "Practical duties" included many topics such as crime scene examination, traffic control, accident investigation, legislation, leadership, report writing, case file preparation, and writing forms, driver training, laws on evidence, court procedures, powers of arrest, search and seizure, conducting interviews, and taking statements, crowd control, sudden death procedures, and court procedures.

Specialist instructors from operational roles were used to train us in search & rescue, use of firearms, batons, and handcuffs, fingerprinting, bushcraft, map

reading and navigation, the inspection of motor vehicles, breathalyzer procedures, road safety, public relations, criminal investigation and holding identification parades, drug identification, and bomb threat procedures.

We were given practical experience with short-term attachments to country police stations and specialist units, including, traffic control, information
bureau, ballistics, criminal investigation branch, fingerprint and photography
sections, and Tasmania Ambulance Service.

Other external activities included outward bound training exercises, including search and rescue activities such as rappelling, retrieving bodies from cliffs
and out of smoke-filled buildings. We spent two weeks in South East Tasmania
bushwalking and practicing map reading and navigation along with other leadership and team-building activities.

We made an official visit to the South Australian Police Academy, which
involved visits to various operational areas such as search and rescue, highway
patrol, and mounted divisions.

We were exposed to other areas that police interacted with, including the
Royal Derwent Hospital psychiatric facility, Parliament House, Magistrates and
Supreme Courts, and the Transport Commission that dealt with the registration
and inspection of motor vehicles.

Public relations activities included escorting the girls in the Hobart regatta
Miss Regatta competition and the youth parliament's opening. In the second
year, we put on some self-defense displays around the State.

We were shown dozens of crime scenes and sudden death photographs to
show us what to expect. Those photos prepared me for seeing a real dead body,
one of my initial fears in the job.

There was a good reason for us looking at the photographs other than the
shock value. Instructors talked through the details in the photos, and lessons
were learned from them. I carried those lessons into the many investigations I did
into sudden death and crime scene investigations.

Some photographs are permanently etched in my mind. One photo of a dead
body with the eye sockets, nose, and mouth full of young maggots almost made
me throw up. I saw plenty of fly-blown carcasses on the farm, and the thought of
a mouthful of maggots was almost too much for me.

Other memorable photos include one woman with her throat cut by a bottle,
pictures of incinerated bodies, bodies mutilated in industrial and road traffic
accidents. Suicide victims with the heads blown off, fully decomposed and fly-
blown bodies, putrefied drowning victims, and axe attack and stabbing victims.

There was not an accidental or deliberate type of death that was not covered by those photographs.

My first encounter with a dead body is now a vivid memory of attending the city mortuary to observe a postmortem examination. This was the first time most of us had seen a dead body, and none of us had watched an autopsy performed.

All of us made it through the postmortem without fainting or throwing up. Some black humor came up, and I confess to one part of it. As the pathologist pulled the deceased's scalp down to skin the skull cap, I said, "Well, that is pulling the wool over his eyes."

It did not make everyone laugh, though. It was a gruesome sight and sound, but it was not much different from watching sheep and cattle being butchered on the farm. The only mental hurdle to get over was that it was a human body, and I had no problem with that at all.

The same day, we visited the pathology museum, where there were all sorts of human body parts in various diseased or injured states on display. It was enough to make Frankenstein's mouth water.

We also visited the mortuary, where numerous bodies were laid out. This 'in your face' exposure to death and injury was, in my opinion, essential to prepare us for what lay ahead. It was the perfect opportunity to decide whether you were right for that part of the job or not.

Initially, I had a great fear of seeing a dead body. I was nervous in the lead up to that day, but when it was over, I knew that I could face whatever came my way in the future, and that is how it turned out for me. I was never afraid of dealing with a body after that experience.

Our training was regularly punctuated by regular theory tests, mid-year and annual theory and practical examinations, and testing for the several qualifications that had to be achieved. I was not aware of it at the time, but I was only just scraping through in the first year of training. I think I still carried my poor attitude to study from my school days.

I learned about my close shave with being dismissed from the Academy in the 1990s while conducting SOG training at the Rokeby Police Academy.

I discovered our cadet course training records stored in cardboard boxes in a basement-type area where we held a tactical assault exercise. I searched for, and found, my personnel file and was shocked to read that I was almost dismissed for poor academic performance at the end of my first year of training.

The report said Bernie McCann supported me in continuing training, saying that I had great potential if I applied myself academically. Although nothing was ever said to me about this, I must have pulled my finger out because I went from the bottom of the course to finish in eighth place.

I never understood why I received the trophy for the "most improved" cadet at graduation, but I do now.

In two years, I graduated from being a prick of a kid at school, a poor student, a bully, an underage smoker, a brawler, and at times a vandal, to being a Constable of the Tasmania Police Force.

Police cadet training and discipline taught me loyalty, teamwork, leadership, self-discipline, personal responsibility, and integrity. These traits are essential for working in dangerous situations and would be developed further over the coming years.

Realistic training that prepares us for the worst that can happen is mentally and physically demanding. Naturally, the more realistic it is, the more stressful it can be. Training that takes short-cuts to avoid the stress factors does not prepare people for the real thing.

However, there is a military saying that "no combat plan survives contact with the enemy," and it applies to the difference between training and real operations. Another favorite saying of mine is "nothing is so bad that it can't get worse."

My adventure was about to begin. Both of those sayings were going to prove to be correct time and time again.

THE BATTLE FOR SELF CONTROL

*"With too much pride, a man cannot learn a thing. In and of itself,
learning teaches you how foolish you are."*

— Criss Jami

Fear of making a mistake or being incompetent can be an obstacle to doing what is right.

I delivered my first death message on Saturday evening, 19th of February 1977. I was on patrol with a slightly more experienced Constable working the 1400 – 2200 hours shift. During that shift, we attended a lost child, a family violence incident, found property, and delivering the death message was the only incident I can remember.

When we received the call to deliver the message, my partner asked if I had given a death message before. When I answered, "No," she replied, "This will be your first then."

I was afraid of being incompetent and unable to deliver the message professionally. I felt that I could not do this correctly and had to ask for help from my partner. She told me to be calm and confident.

The procedure was like this. If both parents are home, ask them both to come to the door because one will offer support to the other on the initial shock. First, ask their names and then ask if they were the parents of (the name of the deceased).

Once I confirmed that the message was being delivered to the right people, I should be direct but as polite as possible. Pussyfooting around the issue only makes it worse for the parents. She warned me that the parents would become very emotional and could collapse at my feet from the shock, and I needed to be prepared for that. "Offer sympathy, but don't overdo it or become emotional yourself," she advised.

Once the parents settled into their grief, I should answer their questions and leave when they had nothing more to say.

I did not want to experience this, but I had no choice. I had to confront the fear I felt and get the job done, regardless of how inadequate I felt.

Delivering the message happened just as my partner said it would. Both parents came to the door, and I could see the look of foreboding on their faces as soon as they saw the uniform. I introduced myself, confirmed their identity, and said, "I am very sorry to have to tell you...."

At that moment, the mother screamed and fell to the floor in a heap. She knew what was coming and did not want to hear it. "No, no, no," she screamed over and over. Her husband bent down to comfort her as I finished, "Your son (first name only) has been killed in a car accident a short time ago."

I felt terrible. The more the mother cried, the more I felt like crying too. I personalized their grief by imagining what it would be like for my mother or father to be getting that message. That was mistake number one. You must not personalize the job.

I went back to the patrol car and sat for a moment. My partner was excellent; she asked how I felt, and I told her, "shit-house." She talked me through the emotions I was feeling and said to me that it was natural to feel that way the first time. She went on to say that wouldn't be the last time I had to deliver that type of message, and I needed to keep my emotions under control. Sage advice.

Calming yourself down when you're feeling frustrated, insulted, threatened, or attacked is more easily said than done. Being able to keep your emotions under control affects how you're perceived by the people around you.

I was so close to crying on this job, and I wondered how on earth was I ever going to be able to control my emotions in the future.

I knew that a lot worse was in store for me.

UNARMED & ILL-EQUIPPED

"If it is important to you, you will find a way. If not, you'll find an excuse."

— Unknown.

The next eye-opening incident occurred 2 months later, on the 25th of April. I worked the 2200 – 0600 shift with one of my course members on beat duty in the city. My diary entry reads, "Call to Somerset re firearms discharged. Two offenders returned to Central and charged." Typical law enforcement understatement, as it turned out.

We received notification from the Watch Sergeant that he would pick us up to attend a shots-fired incident in a neighboring suburb.

It took ten minutes to get to the scene. On the way, the Sergeant informed us that shots from a high-powered rifle had been fired into a house. The shots had been fired from a scrubby area between the highway and beachfront; that was where we would start searching for them.

My partner and I were both armed with snub-nose Smith and Wesson .38 pistols.

It is bad enough going to any gunfight but, those pistols against a high-powered rifle in an open area was bullshit. However, we had to do it and hope for the best.

But the Sergeant had a plan! The first thing he did was order me to hand over my pistol to him. He set up a command post in the car while Paul and I went looking for the gun. Praise the Lord he left me with a torch, though.

Sarge parked the patrol car facing directly into the scrub area with the headlights on high beam. He deployed me to the front and Paul to the right in a flanking movement to flush the two offenders out.

Are you getting an idea of how stupid this was?

We did as we were ordered, and I made it to a wire fence at the end of a grassed area of about 10 meters in width before it reached a railway line. Beyond that were trees.

I took cover behind a railway line fence post. I thought that the gunmen had me in their sights as I tried to shrink myself to fit into the fence post and hide from the glare of the patrol car headlights. I had never felt terror like I felt at that moment. Seriously, I had never been so scared in my life as I was at that moment.

The Sergeant did not bother getting out of the car. He shouted his orders across the road for us to get over the fence and flush the offenders out.

I was too junior in the job to tell him to "get fucked, you come and do it." What he was asking us to do was insanity and I make that judgment on what I know now after 40 years of experience.

Paul and I got through the fence and started walking towards each other, scanning the area between us for the gunmen. Suddenly, there they were, lying in the grass on their faces — one of them laying with the rifle in his hands.

Paul covered them both with his pistol, and I rushed in on top of the one with the rifle and put him in a bear hug that Grizzly Adams would be proud of.

Fortunately, 'old mate' had run out of piss and vinegar and was playing possum. We were able to restrain both culprits without any great struggle. Neither of them put up any fight or resistance at all.

However, the rifle was locked and loaded with some high-powered hunting ammunition. I don't recall the caliber, other than it was a European caliber and uncommon in Tasmania.

I started to think:

- I should not have to give up my pistol to anyone who will put me into the firing line.
- A .38 Smith and Wesson is not good enough.

MANHUNT

*Avoiding danger is no safer in the long run than outright exposure. The
fearful are caught as often as the bold.*

— Helen Keller

In August 1980, a man was murdered over an argument about $60. He was shot
in the chest 6 times outside a hotel in East Devonport.

The suspect was a well-known violent person; and he went on the run for six
days.

The manhunt was on. Overtime city! Every available officer from neighboring stations was deployed on the manhunt, including the Armed Offenders
Squad from the capital city.

General duties police and detectives in those days were issued with the Smith
and Wesson snub-nose .38 revolver.

The Armed Offender Squad had bigger guns, mostly acquired from the Ballistics Section seized and surrendered firearms museum. They included 12-gauge
shotguns, .30 cal. M1 carbines, and maybe a Thompson sub-machine gun or two.

One day on the manhunt, we searched a pine plantation where a person
fitting the suspect's description was reportedly seen. About twenty or more
officers were lined up and sent off into the trees to flush out the suspect, who,
by the way, had threatened to gun down any police that came after him. I
looked along the line and saw officers had armed themselves with their private
firearms, including hunting rifles and shotguns. It looked like a posse out of a
western movie.

I did not know what was supposed to happen, so I treated it like a kangaroo
hunt. If it moved, I'd try and shoot it. However, the fact that the kangaroo could
shoot me first was not lost in my thinking.

Understand this. In those days, we had to call on the suspect to surrender
and we could not shoot until we were shot at first. Even then, our rules of engage-
ment meant we had to fire warning shots!

As we walked through the young pines, my eyes were trying to pierce through the undergrowth, hoping to see the suspect before he shot me. I imagined him hidden in the grass, aiming his rifle at me. The hair was standing up on the back of my neck. My blood was running cold. I felt that there was no way we could stop him from shooting first because he could be hiding anywhere.

That day I participated in the most stressful diddly-bop in a pine forest that I have ever experienced. I knew damn well I wouldn't do that again.

Later that day, we received information that the murderer was seen at a house in a nearby small town. My partner and I were given the job of going to the house and searching it alone. We had no training on how to go about it. All we had were our two revolvers and whatever common sense we could muster between us.

Our plan to check the house was amateurish. My partner, Errol, approached from one side and me from the other. I waited for the sound of breaking glass as the suspect thrust the barrel of his rifle through a window to shoot at us. I ran crouch as low as I could along the fence line towards the house. My eyes were glued to the windows at the front of the house. I knew that if I had to shoot with my revolver, I had no chance of hitting the target because I hadn't fired the bloody thing for over four years.

We crept along the front of the house, ducking under the windows. Was he watching us? Was he waiting until we passed under the window to shoot us in the back? What could I do if I heard the window break as he pointed the barrel of his rifle to shoot? I simply did not know what I was going to do.

We made it to the front door. I felt a little safer for some strange reason. Errol knocked on the door, but there was no answer. Nobody was home.

The terror I felt during that time was real. I don't know what Errol felt because we both talked about it afterward as if it was all in a day's work. It was false bravado on my part.

The point is that we had no choice other than to do that search. Backing out of it, not doing the job, was simply not an option. I had to force myself to go forward and through it, regardless of how scared I was that I could be killed.

We searched four other premises that day through to 0200 hours and several more in the following days as we helped to try and flush the suspect out. The warning that he would shoot any police that tried to apprehend him was front and foremost in everyone's mind.

My fear gradually became less as each search proved fruitless. It did not go away entirely though, I could feel my heart thumping in my chest, and my breathing felt restricted on each search. The adrenalin rush did not stop until the end of each day, washed away with several beers.

The experience of searching for an armed and dangerous person like this hammered into me how inadequately I was trained and equipped for these high-risk operations.

I became more determined to learn more about dealing with active shooters, but the first thing I did was buy myself a Mossberg 12 gauge 8-shot pump-action riot gun. I wanted to be better armed if I was going to have to do this sort of shit, and the .38 special was not going to cut it as far as I was concerned.

Life in the Criminal Investigation Branch turned out to be the adventure of a lifetime. I did not know what I was going to be dealing with on any day. The adrenalin rush came suddenly, and it came often. Those were the days.

My diary entries range from office duties and inquiries to dealing with rape and murder and the occasional interstate extradition or court appearance. I was never tired of the work – I loved it.

I lived for the job and I had become addicted to the adrenaline rush and excitement that came with danger.

As I said earlier, my oath of office meant more to me than anything else in the world. I live by it today. Even though I am not employed by Tasmania Police, I am 'protect and serve' to the core.

Mentally and physically, a law enforcement officer must be prepared for anything every minute of every day. The best, worst, mundane, and most dangerous situations can occur in an instant.

There were times I was sitting at my desk working on a case, and the boss would rush into the office and report some serious crime that needed to be attended to. A detective's thinking goes from zero to 100 miles an hour in the blink of an eye. Your adrenaline spikes and your concentration on what lays ahead becomes intense.

It wasn't a job. It was an adventure out on the edge. Somewhere I heard the saying, 'if you aren't living on the edge, you are taking up too much room.' In that case, I don't think circumstances allowed me to take up too much room.

Truly, my worst fear, the one that would be the hardest to live with if it eventuated, was stuffing up or not doing a good job. Getting killed or hurt did not feature too high on my radar back then. To be honest, within a few years of being a detective, I had developed a bad attitude. I thought I was bulletproof.

My attitude changed over the next few years. After I was promoted, I had greater responsibility for the safety of others. I knew I had to become more skilled in planning and leadership, especially taking people into the dangerous types of situations that I enjoyed.

Up until this time, life was a walk in the park compared to the next few years. Shit got serious after I was promoted and transferred to the George Town Criminal Investigation Branch in 1985.

THE DANGER OF A CLOSED MIND

Normal people run away from the gunfire. A police officer has no choice.
He must run towards it.

January 1986 was a full-on month for the George Town CIB. I assisted at a nasty fatal road traffic accident on the 9th, investigated numerous burglaries, investigated and arrested a filthy-dirty old bastard for an indecent assault on a 6-year-old girl, performed close personal protection for the visiting Prime Minister, and provided investigation support to the Launceston CIB regarding the murder of Caroline Hope. I worked long hours and clocked up 27 hours overtime in 4 days.

In the days before mobile telephones and pagers, the old hand-held phone was the only means of after-hours contact. I had two telephones in my house, one beside the bed and one in the study.

How I hate telephones! If a psychologist told me today that my aversion to telephones was a PTSD problem, I would throw my hands up and confess.

Working as a Detective, whether I was sound asleep, having a dinner party, working in the garden, or reading a book, it was always bad news when that fucking phone rang. My typical greeting on answering the telephone became, "What's wrong?"

Nothing fucks up a dinner party like being told that you have to investigate the rape of a 5-year-old girl.

Your barbeque quickly turns to shit when you have to go investigate someone who has blown their head off.

Being called off the golf course on a Saturday morning to go deal with some 20-year-old that got drunk last night and shot himself in bed ruins your handicap.

On Sunday, the 2nd of February, I was on a rostered day off. The telephone rang at 0145 hours, and the call went something like this.

Dispatcher: Sergeant, I don't want you to be alarmed, but there is an armed offender in the vicinity of your house. He has already shot at police and is at large. We are receiving reports of gunshots in your area. Constables Morgan and Nesbit have returned to the station and require your attendance.

Me: Where did this all happen.

Dispatcher: The officers were patrolling behind Gray's Hotel. A male person stepped into the bottle shop driveway and fired two shots at the police car. They hit reverse gear and backed off to return to the station to get your assistance.

I told the dispatcher to instruct the officers to be standing at the front door of the station and be ready to open it as soon as they saw me running across the road. I planned to be running at full speed and was not going to slow down until I was in the reception area.

I quickly dressed in some casual clothes, grabbed my pistol, and sprinted the 200 meters from my house to the station.

Not knowing where the gunman was, who he was, or what it was all about gave me an adrenaline rush. Was I going to get shot in the back? I had to run past where he had already fired at the police. Was he going to step out in front of me and shoot? Was I going to have to kill someone tonight? These are just some of the questions flying through my mind as I ran towards the station.

The officers opened the door as I crossed the pavement and hit the door at full speed. I can still picture the look on the faces of the two officers.

They looked shocked by the situation. Justifiably so.

By this time in my career, my confidence to handle violence; and my knowledge of the law was high. I felt the excitement of what lay ahead, and I was conscious of the physical effects of adrenaline flowing. My mind was switched on and focused as I slowed my breathing after the sprint to the station.

The briefing the officers gave me was that they were routinely patrolling behind the hotel (which was closed). They were suddenly ambushed by what appeared to be a youth armed with a .22 caliber rifle. Neither was hurt, and as far as I can remember, no shots hit the police car, or a bullet may have ricocheted off the windscreen without causing any damage.

They believed the offender was a 14-year-old boy and gave me his name.

That was the first curveball for the night.

I had mentally rehearsed an active shooter scenario many times since that first occasion, but not one involving a child. Being forced into killing a child, regardless of the justification for it, had never crossed my mind before this. I was going to have to deal with this situation very carefully.

The gunman's age was a serious tactical problem to deal with. Police weren't permitted to interview a person under sixteen years of age without a parent or guardian present. But here I was about to confront one that I might have to kill.

In this case, the priorities were simple and firmly fixed in my mind. My safety first, public second, the other officers third, and the kid last of all. If this went pear-shaped, I needed to make sure I had the legality of my actions squared away nice and tight.

During the briefing, we could hear calls over the police radio of reports of motorists being shot at on the main road into town, not far from the police station.

Clearly, this was becoming a more dangerous situation; and we had to get moving. I said that we would all go in the one marked uniform car. My idea was to attract the gunman to us and divert him away from other motorists.

My colleagues did not like that idea and briefly protested accordingly. I reminded them that he was only 14 years old, using a .22 rifle, and he had already missed them once, plus if he shot at us, I would be shooting back at him!

I went to my office, took my Mossberg shotgun, loaded it with oo buckshot, and put extra cartridges in my pocket. Carrying plenty of ammunition was as good a confidence builder as wearing body armor.

I understood the officers' reluctance to go back out and confront this situation, and I hope the reader does too.

When a police officer goes into an active shooter situation, he or she is taking a walk through the valley of the shadow of death.

We drove to the gunman's last known location. As we arrived, we received a report over the radio that shots were being fired. Someone was trying to break into a house on Conrad Avenue. We drove to that location and parked one street back, so we could move in on foot. My plan was for me to enter Conrad Avenue, and the two uniform officers were to approach over the back fences from different directions.

Your best chance of coping with chaos in a crisis is to have a pre-determined plan. My plan was textbook; isolate, contain, evacuate, communicate, negotiate, use force as a last resort. An old warrior saying is that "no combat plan survives contact with the enemy". Ain't that the truth!

As I entered Conrad Avenue, I heard two shots being fired. I was able to pinpoint the gunman's location by the shouting and the sound of breaking glass. I was able to tell from the sound of the gunshots that a .22 caliber rifle was being fired.

A .22 rifle did not worry me too much if there was a reasonable distance between it and me. I had hunted with one for many years and knew plenty of examples where people had survived being shot with one. On the other hand, I knew of plenty who had died from a .22 bullet. It is the assassin's weapon of choice.

It was a 50/50 risk. I could afford to be a bit bolder than I would if I was going up against a high-powered weapon, especially when it was in the hands of a young person. I was a big man back then. I was fit and heavy from bodybuilding. I thought that maybe a .22 wouldn't make it to my vital organs. It was a risk I was prepared to take.

However, my theory and plan did not quite work out as well as I thought it would.

Using the cover of darkness and shrubs, I ran down the opposite side of the street. I saw the youth kicking at the house's front door, and he was demanding to be let in. A woman was screaming inside the house.

I had plenty of experience dealing with angry people to know that they can react with violence spontaneously if you surprise them. I had to find some cover before making him aware of my presence or run the risk of him catching me out in the open and shooting at me.

I found cover under a painter's trailer, which was parked on the nature strip opposite where he was. I crawled underneath it and took cover beside a wheel. The shotgun was already locked and loaded. I settled myself and took aim before calling out to him.

If he got lucky and shot at me, I knew that I was going to have to give him a gut-full of buckshot before he got off a second shot. I could see the headlines, "Detective kills a 14-year old boy." I was in a tight spot.

In a crisis, humans fall back on three basic instincts when they are threatened, which are fight, flight, or freeze. The question for me was which option he was likely to choose. The answer was, "any one of the three."

Hoping for the best, I thought it was more likely he would 'freeze.' My sudden appearance might confuse him and give me the chance to talk him out of doing something stupid.

He could choose 'flight' and run. I did not like the thought of chasing a kid with a loaded rifle. I hoped that the other two officers were in position at the end of the cul-de-sac to cut him off or at least distract him.

I called out the boy's name and identified myself. I told him to drop the weapon and talk to me.

He chose 'fight.' Talk about pouring petrol onto a fire! His response was immediate and insanely aggressive. He spun around and aimed the rifle where he must have thought the sound of my voice came from. He was close, but not close enough for me to believe he could shoot me.

He shouted out, "Where are you, you cunt. I've got a bullet here for you." I quickly interrupted him hoping to stop him from coming closer. I shouted firmly, "just put the gun down so we can talk. There's no need for anyone to get hurt. I am armed, and I'll shoot you if you come any closer."

That was another part of the plan that did not survive contact with the enemy.

The situation was going from bad to worse very rapidly. The boy came searching for me, gun up, and ready to shoot. Suddenly, I was in a 'shoot, don't shoot' situation — a cop's worse nightmare.

Being only fourteen years old made the problem far worse than I could ever expect. A fucking fourteen-year-old boy deliberately taking me on with a rifle rocked me to the core. To be honest, I went into this situation hoping that the kid would give himself up quickly.

I could tell that he was scanning the area where I was located but he couldn't see me. I was in the shadow and under the trailer.

He showed absolutely no sign of fear or willingness to stop or talk. It was plain as paint (another pun intended) that he was gunning for me and closing distance between us fast. I thought, "this idiot is seriously trying to gun me down."

Although I was surprised momentarily, my thinking went into over-drive.

I did the legal thinking first. Using the poker machine analogy, this was the first wheel to spin. Every section in Chapter IV of the Criminal Code is on this wheel. I knew the law on the use of force backward. The situation was on the very brink of justifying me to shoot him down, but this wheel keeps on spinning until the others lined up.

The second wheel to spin was the continuum of use of force. There are 15 options to spin on this wheel. I created a problem because I was carrying the shotgun, which was not a police issue firearm. The shotgun was a wild card.

The next wheel was the 'consequences for me wheel.' Living through this was good for me, but I knew that the Police Department wouldn't give a fuck about that. If I killed this kid, it would definitely make the TV news, and the Department was not likely to go easy on me. If the Department couldn't get me for unlawful use of force, they would fry my arse for using a private firearm.

I was now in a situation where my judgment was being affected by the 'wild card' - carrying a personally owned firearm. I was confident in the law, but I still had to think about the trouble I would be in if I blew a 14-year-old in half with oo buckshot out of a Mossberg riot gun.

Many who have been through life-threatening conditions talk about something happening in slow motion. However, the reality is that your brain is processing information much faster than usual.

I had learned how to simplify things very fast and prioritize action through studying crisis decision making and by practice in training exercises. My ability was being put to the test once again in this case.

Let me try and relate my thinking in this situation, but before you ask, "how can you remember," let me assure you that you never forget this sort of thing.

His body language, the way he pointed the rifle, and his language were crystal clear. He would shoot me if he found me. He was about ten meters away and walking in my direction. A few more steps and he would see me. If I moved or spoke, he would find me.

It was deathly quiet except for him shouting. I felt calm, but my thoughts felt as if they were screaming in my head.

I aimed the shotgun at his chest. I imagined the shot leaving the barrel and hitting him. The plastic carrier that contained the 9mm lead pellets would still be intact at the time of impact. Those nine lead balls would be held together as they entered his chest. I was going to blow him in half if I shot at that range.

I stayed still and quiet. Part of my thinking turned to the other officers. Where the fuck *were* they? I was expecting one of them to walk into the situation. If the kid pointed the rifle at them, I would have to shoot because I had no doubt that he was ready to kill. All I needed at that stage was a diversion.

I took up the first pressure on the trigger. If his eyes locked onto me, I was going to shoot.

The consequences of me killing the kid flashed through my mind again like a bolt of lightning. I did not want to kill him but couldn't see a way out of it. He was starting to crouch down and look in my direction through the shadows.

This was going to be close. I thought I would shout out "drop it, or I shoot," at the last second, but I expected that the youth would immediately target me and shoot anyway. I was ready to shoot as soon as I spoke. My thinking settled, and I became calm. Well, here goes, I thought.

He pointed the rifle at me, but he hadn't seen me.

My options, and their consequences, went through my mind like a flashing strobe light — no panic, just quick thinking. Shoot, don't shoot; live or die; wait a bit more; could I risk surviving being shot with a .22?

Critical incident stress can include symptoms of being dazed, confused, or helpless, but I felt none of these.

Human hearing, vision, and time perception can become distorted in crisis situations. I believe the distortion depends on what you are most focused on at any point in time.

It felt like my mind was screaming at me, trying to make me panic.

"He's only fucking 14, you're going to cut him in half."

"You're going to have to shoot him."

"He can't see me yet; I won't shoot until he sees me."

"When he steps onto the nature strip, I'll shoot."

Slowing my breathing kept any feeling of panic at bay. I chose to wait until he either saw me or got so close that he couldn't miss if he pulled the trigger.

I concluded that I would not shoot until the barrel of his rifle was pointed at me, and I was sure that he could see me.

The kid was waving the rifle from side to side as he got to the middle of the street.

I was totally immobile and held my breath as he approached to within 5 meters of my position. He was on the hunt for me.

Suddenly, he stopped walking and came out of his crouch. He shouted, "Where are the rest of you cunts? Come on out where I can see you."

He was suddenly scared. He was out in the open and must have realized that he was exposed. There was fear in his voice now, and his body language changed from attack to defense.

Suddenly, he started running down the street towards an open park. "Dammit," I thought, "can this get any fucking worse."

I ran after him shouting, "stop or I'll shoot." This was not the only time that I found that threatening to shoot a running crook made them run faster. He ran faster.

I had gained ground on him as he entered the park, and in that time, I got the feeling that he probably was not as determined to shoot at me as he was a second or so before.

After running about 50-meters, he stopped out in the open in the park. He turned towards me and aimed the rifle at me. I was on the footpath in front of the last house that bordered the park. I switched direction and slammed up against a paling fence.

I knew the fence was not going to stop a .22 bullet, but if he shot me through the fence, I would still have a good chance of surviving.

But things were about to take a turn for the worse.

Another youth, about 17-years old and drunk, came walking through the park to interrupted proceedings. He sauntered up to the kid and said, "Hey (name), what's going on?"

The boy rammed the barrel of the rifle under the youth's chin and called out to me, "Now I've got a hostage!"

That left me with the problem of having to worry about the safety of another person. I was starting to wonder what else could go wrong, and if I would get the situation under control at all.

Even though the youth was a drug-taking criminal, I couldn't allow him to get shot. OK, to be honest, I did not think it would be a great loss, but it wouldn't look good on my resume if that happened.

My thinking changed fast. The first two principles of isolate and contain the incident was looking more difficult as the incident progressed. Unless all alone and unaided, I could surround the little prick, there was not much I could do to contain him. So, I exposed myself to him to draw his attention to me instead of the knucklehead he had standing on tippy-toes at the end of the barrel of his rifle.

At that time, John, one of the uniform officers, turned up at my side. While we spoke quickly about how we could get the situation under control, the boy called out, demanding a cigarette.

John said he had cigarettes. We decided to give him a cigarette, but not a lighter, hoping to buy more negotiating time. I called out to the kid that he could have a smoke, but he had to come and get it.

The kid countered that by saying that he would send the hostage over to get one. He kept the rifle pointed at the youth as he walked about 20 yards to our position. "Don't do anything stupid, or I'll shoot him," he yelled.

When the youth arrived at our position, it was evident that he was drunk or stoned and oblivious to the situation's seriousness.

The uniform officer handed the youth a cigarette, and I told him to stay calm and don't do anything stupid. He slurred out the words, "She'll be right; I can sort him out." I tried to talk him out of doing anything and let us talk him out of it, but the boy was demanding the youth to go back immediately, or he would shoot. All I could do was tell the youth to get back to him and not do anything stupid.

If the situation was not bad enough already, it took another bloody turn for the worse!

The youth had a cigarette lighter and offered to light the boy's cigarette. As the lighter flared, the youth grabbed the rifle barrel with both hands and started to wrestle over it. As they wrestled back and forward, I ran out from behind the fence and charged towards the pair.

The boy saw me coming and let go of the rifle and ran. I was able to run him down quickly and place him under arrest after a scuffle that he had no hope of winning. Finally, it was over.

It turned out that the boy thought his father had been arrested by the police and locked up, and his intention was to break his father out of jail. I shit you not!

He had gone home and taken his father's rifle, intent on holding up the police and forcing them to release his father. As he left his home, two women pulled up in a car next door, and he stole their car at gunpoint but crashed it in the town center. He walked towards the nearby police station and fired shots at the police car as it patrolled through a car park.

The whole situation took four hours to resolve, although the hostage situation lasted only ten minutes. I charged the boy with several crimes and offenses, but he was not prosecuted.

Several lessons came out of this experience for me. The fact that the boy was only 14 years old played too much on my mind as he was approaching me with intent to shoot. I am glad I did not have to shoot him, but the fact that he took a hostage troubled me for a long time.

What if he had shot the hostage deliberately or accidentally? I could have prevented that from happening, but it would have cost the boy's life and me a whole heap of paperwork. I am sure I could have justified shooting him, but my plan was working up until the hostage came along.

This situation was resolved with a lot of luck involved. The scenario made me think about the legality of using lethal force when a person was escaping custody when there was a risk of them taking a hostage.

On the face of it, the law said that you couldn't use lethal force to prevent an escape from custody. However, I could see no other option in the scenario I had in my mind.

I went back to study the law in more detail, looking for an answer, and found it. In simple terms, if there were reasonable grounds to believe that a person's life was in immediate danger, lethal force could be justified.

My scenario eventuated on the 5th of June 1988 while attempting to arrest a man for rape and murder in the Ringarooma district of North East Tasmania.

KNOW WHERE YOU STAND

"Doing the right thing is not the problem. Knowing what the right thing is, that's the challenge."

Lyndon B. Johnson

This case involved a murder stemming from a broken relationship. The murderer's girlfriend was in a car with her new boyfriend. The murderer opened the car door and stabbed the boyfriend in the heart with a fillet knife. He dragged the woman, drenched in blood, over the bleeding body, and dragged her into his car.

He drove her to a remote property on a mixed forest and pasture property. On the way there, he called into his house to collect a rifle.

He took the girl to the base of a heavily wooded mountain. He told her that he planned to kill her and dump her body because she witnessed the murder.

He raped the girl, but before he could kill her, she talked him out of it by concocting a story that she would tell the police that a hitchhiker had murdered her boyfriend.

The murderer bought the story and dropped the girl back in the town where she went to the nearest house and called the police.

I interviewed her at the house, and after doing what was necessary for her care, I took a team of Detectives to the killer's house.

We forced entry into the house and found the killer in bed. None of us knew the fellow by sight, but we had an old photostat picture of him that we obtained from the department's records section.

We asked the fellow's name, and he gave us another name. I asked him where (name) was, and he replied, "I don't know. He hasn't come home yet."

I was not buying it. I said, "I believe you are (name), and you are under arrest for murder." As I was saying that I reached for his arm, but he took off out the door.

I took off after him.

It was a cold, dismal day, and everything outside was wet. He vaulted the paling fence around the yard like it was not there. I was so close to him that I had to measure my step to avoid his flying feet and brace to jump the fence. That did not work out as I imagined it would.

As I braced my right foot, it slipped on the wet grass, and I fell in a heap at the bottom of the fence. I scrambled to my feet and vaulted the fence, but one of the other detectives had got close, and I accidentally kicked him in the face as I went over the top.

By this time, the killer had about thirty meters break on me, running in the direction of a neighboring farmhouse. I had fears that he would break into the house and take someone hostage. There was no doubt that there would be firearms in there as well.

All the Detectives had joined the chase. Some were running behind me and a pair in a car drove along the road. No one had to be told that we had to stop the killer from getting to the farmhouse.

This was another situation where I had to make a fast decision to shoot or not.

My past experiences that involved fast-moving situations had got me to the point of making fast decisions using a traffic light system. It involves rapidly processing the information you have about the situation and deciding on a course of action like this. Red light means 'don't do it,' orange light means 'wait,' and Greenlight means 'do it.'

I had a green light to shoot to kill because if he made it to the farmhouse, he could obtain a firearm and take a hostage. I was going to kill him to protect the life of whoever was in that house.

I had the Detective Special .38, which, I think you realize by now, is totally useless to shoot anyone any more than 10 meters away. I needed it to be a perfect shot and have plenty of luck to drop a man running at full speed from a distance, starting at about fifty yards. At that range, trying to put a bullet in him was like firing artillery shells.

The first two shots I fired were warning shots. I realized my mistake immediately. Firing those two shots was a result of my special operations training, where we fired double taps. I only had three rounds left in the pistol and no spares.

I knew my pistol well and understood the ballistics of the bullets I was using. They were over-powered for the snub-nose barrel and only suitable for very close range against a human target.

I aimed high over the killer's right shoulder, leading him by about ten meters. That shot went over his right shoulder and chewed up the mud about where I had aimed. He picked up speed.

I shifted my aim and anticipated hitting him between the shoulder blades. That fourth shot just missed him at waist height slightly to the right.

Although the elevation was good for the fourth shot, the killer put more distance between us. Another quick adjustment was needed.

I aimed my last shot over his head, about twenty meters in front of him, to allow for the fall of the shot. It hit the ground just behind his right foot and sprayed the back of his leg with mud.

Interestingly, I don't remember hearing my shots, but I can still visualize the three that I aimed at him. The reason for that is I was using my visual senses to aim, fire, and adjust.

At least one other detective fired a couple of shots, but by this time, the killer had got too close to the house to shoot safely.

Two detectives had got into their car and cut the man off from entering the house. They captured him without much struggle because he was exhausted from running.

He was charged and convicted of murder and served over 30 years in prison.

Under cross-examination by his defense attorney in the trial, I was asked about five questions about my decision to use lethal force. My answers were based on my belief that he was heading toward the neighboring house where he could take a hostage and obtain a firearm. My concern was that he killed a person not long before, had threatened to kill a witness, and that he would be prepared to kill again. My answers justified the use of lethal force on that occasion.

My decision was made easy because I had imagined this scenario and studied everything I needed to know if it happened in reality. I could make a fast decision without any fear of being found guilty of breaking the law and being confident that I could justify my action.

Other lessons to be learned were the stupidity of firing warning shots and firearms training not matching operational work reality.

At that time, police were taught to fire a warning shot before shooting at a person. General duties police firearms training was nothing more than target practice. However, the SOG training was as close to reality as we could get at that time. I was highly trained in special operations tactics. However, in this case, I was not working in a special ops environment. Conflict everywhere.

The warning shots I fired at the killer were instinctive but inappropriate. I left myself three bullets to drop him from an unrealistic range for that weapon — wrong training and inappropriate firearm for this situation.

I mentioned early the fear of being made look a fool. Although I did not give that a thought in the heat of the moment, I copped a lot of shit-stirring from the other detectives about being a lousy shot afterwards. "I thought you blokes in the SOG were supposed to be able to shoot," was the joke of the day.

The lessons I learned were not wasted. I used this case to help justify the change in departmental policy on firearms. Eventually, SOG personnel were permitted to carry their personal issued 9mm Browning Hi-power pistols on general duty.

Later, I was given the task of reviewing the Department's policy on arming general duties police and making recommendations for the Commissioners' consideration. Consequently, 9mm Glock pistols became the standard issue for Tasmania Police.

SURPRISE COMES FROM THE UNEXPECTED

Say what you will, but you are never ready for the surprise attack.

— Sarah Dessen

My partner and I worked late one evening to provide support to Australian Federal Police officers on a job. It was a mundane job to interview a female suspect over a pension fraud. They had her in custody at the station to interview her.

My partner and I were working in our offices near the police station's back door when we heard a knock on the back door.

The doors were glass, so as I walked up to them, I saw a rough-looking bloke, obviously very angry, banging at the door with his two fists. It was the suspect's husband.

I unlocked and opened the door and asked what he wanted. He said he knew the 'feds' had his wife at the station, and he demanded to see her. I told him I would get one of them to come to the door to talk to him.

I told the feds that the husband wanted to see them, and one of them went out the back to speak to the husband, and I returned to my office.

Not long after, the officer came to my office and told me that the suspect's husband had become violent and threatened to break into the police station. He wanted his wife released immediately.

The officer asked me to deal with him, so he could get back to the interview.

I was happy to oblige and figured that the worst that could come out of it would be that the husband would refuse to leave, and I would have to arrest him.

Anticipating that arresting him would involve a physical struggle, I emptied my pockets and left my pistol on my desk. There was no point taking the risk of him taking it off me during a fight. I told my partner that I was going out to sort the bloke out.

I went to the back door with the federal cop, unlocked it, and stepped up to the bloke to try and talk to him. But, as I walked towards him, I heard the station door lock. I looked over my shoulder to see the Fed walking back into the police station.

"You bastard," I thought. He caused the problem and he was not hanging around to back me up if I needed it. He had locked me out of the fucking station. I couldn't believe it!

At the same time, I was now facing a furious man demanding to see his wife and have her released from custody. I explained to him that that was not going to happen, and the best thing he could do was go home and wait for her to return after the Feds had finished their interview with her.

I did not know whether the husband was on drugs or not, but his anger was irrational and intense. He was not listening to a word I said. I threatened to arrest him if he did not leave the station, but he replied that he would not leave, and I was not going to stop him from getting into the police station.

He walked towards his motor vehicle. It was a beat-up a red station wagon with no rear window. I could tell that he wasn't planning to drive off, so I stood back, expecting him to be getting a runup to charge at me. However, he reached into the back of his car and pulled out an axe.

He gripped it with both hands and swung it up over his shoulder. He walked towards me aiming to swing the axe at me. His face was enraged as he snarled through gritted teeth, "Let's see how you like this," he snarled.

I had not met this person before, but I had heard about him. He was a brawler, known to be violent, and here I was, facing off with him, totally unarmed and trapped at the back of the police station. I had no idea how to defend myself against an axe attack and I realized I was in a whole heap of trouble.

Still facing him, I walked backwards towards the windows where my offices were, intending to calmly call out to my partner without provoking the husband to launch his attack. I called out my partner's name three or four times with increasing urgency on each occasion. Finally, my partner looked out through the window blinds, and I said, "Get out here now, and bring my pistol with you."

He was only a few meters away from me by that time, and the axe was raised above his head. I was fucked if I did nothing. I continued to step backwards to maintain a gap between us that would enable me to defend myself.

I heard my partner running in the station, and the next thing was he came out of the back door and ran to my side with my pistol in his hand. His eyes were open wide and there was a look of shock on his face, but I bet the look on mine was worse.

I grabbed my pistol from him, cocked it, and pointed it at the bloke's head, saying something like, "Let's see how you like some of this. Get in your car and fuck off before I blow your fucking head off". That stopped him in his tracks.

I started walking towards him; and he started to walk backwards towards his car, axe still raised above his head. I aimed the pistol between his eyes and advanced in the most aggressive pose I could muster. I could see he was having second thoughts. I was deadly serious. If I was a killer, I could have shot him and justified it.

As he got to the back of his car, he cast his eyes between me and it. Finally, he tossed the axe into the back of his car, got in the driver's seat, saying, "You haven't heard the last of this," and then he drove away.

My partner and I returned to our office and spent a bit of time discussing how gutless and weak as piss the Feds were. I remember the now familiar feeling of the adrenaline rush subsiding. I needed a beer or two.

As a result of that experience, I studied how to defend myself against an axe, baseball bat, and other types of extended weapons. I also learned to never take my firearm off when going into an altercation.

To overcome the risk of having my pistol taken off me in a struggle, I learned weapon retention techniques and practiced them frequently.

My concern with weapon retention became a bit of a joke among other officers who were not so tactically minded. Often enough, one would walk up behind me and touch the butt of my pistol just to watch my reaction.

Another unexpected attack came soon after, but I was better prepared for this one.

One afternoon, two of the station's uniform officers informed me that a known criminal had been heard threatening to kill one of them. They were quite concerned about it. Not being one to ignore these types of threats, my partner and I immediately got in our car and drove to the suspect's home.

Upon arrival, I saw the suspect kneeling on the ground beside his car's open passenger door in the driveway. He appeared to be working on the vehicle.

As we pulled up, he looked over his shoulder and saw us.

Things happened very quickly from that moment. His face became very aggressive and he reached into the car. I considered that he could be reaching for a weapon. I rapidly opened my door, drew my pistol, and rushed across the lawn towards the suspect.

As I got close to him, he rose suddenly to his feet and turned towards me. He had armed himself with a large screwdriver. He started to make a threatening move towards us but stopped as soon as he recognized that there was a pistol pointed at him. I snarled at him to drop the screwdriver. He hesitated, and I could see that he was weighing up the odds, but he dropped the weapon after a moment's hesitation.

We spoke to the suspect in his yard and, in a persuasive manner, encouraged him to think again about making threats about attacking police officers in the future. I never heard from that bloke again after that, so our little talk with him must have had the desired effect.

This situation impressed on me the notion to never take a threat lightly and never approach a situation thinking that all was normal.

ALWAYS TRUST YOUR GUT INSTINCTS

A scout is never taken by surprise; he always knows what to do when anything unexpected happens.

— Robert Baden-Powell

On Thursday, 14 January 1988, I was called to a house in George Town to respond to a young man was threatening to shoot himself. When I arrived at the address, the uniform Police Sergeant was standing at the front door. I could see another officer in the short hallway. As I approached the front door, I heard, "Get Dyson here. I only want to see Dyson."

A red flag flashed in my mind and I was immediately suspicious. I did not know the address or the person inside and I did not know anything about the situation.

Going into any situation where a firearm is involved is a risk. I needed a moment to go through the OODA loop.

OODA is a decision-making tool, the anacronym for observe, orientate, decide, act. I had done the observing part, now it was time to orientate myself to the situation before making a decision about what action to take.

So, instead of walking in like a hero to save the day, I signaled the Sergeant to say nothing and beckoned him to come to me on the street.

I asked him who the person inside the house was, and he told me his name. I asked the Sergeant, Ted, why he wanted to see me, and he replied that it was the first time he had mentioned it. They had been trying to get the fellow to lay down his gun for some time, but he seemed to be waiting to make up his mind to shoot himself.

Suicide investigation is one of the functions of criminal investigators. The primary purpose is to determine the cause of death and whether a murder was involved. Having investigated many suicides, I knew the importance of establishing a motive. I was also aware that a family history of suicide can be relevant to a person committing suicide. I needed more information about the young man before I got involved.

Ted told me that the person's wife was in the house next door, so I decided to speak to her first and leave the negotiating with him.

The next-door neighbor invited me into the house. The man's wife was sitting at the kitchen table looking through the window at her house. She was in a distressed state, but I still had to ask her some sensitive questions if I was to have a chance of talking her husband out of blowing his brains out.

The fact that he had explicitly asked for me interested me most to start with. I was not a popular detective amongst the town's troublemakers, so I wondered if I had crossed paths with this person before. Was he a threat to me?

His wife told me that she knew of no reason why he would want to kill himself, and there was no history of suicide in his family. She said that he had never got over the suicide of his best friend some years earlier and often talked about it. He had never mentioned my name to her.

I immediately recognized the suicide she was talking about. It was one of the most unusual ones I had investigated because of the number of methods the bloke used before he finally succeeded. It happened in another town about five years earlier.

The victim killed himself after a breakdown in his relationship with my sister. That connection was enough to warn me that I might make matters worse if I became involved in the negotiation.

While I was still talking to the wife, I was able to see through the window that the two uniform officers had the husband in handcuffs and were walking him to the police car. They carried a double-barrel shotgun and had obviously resolved the situation.

I saw the Sergeant on the following Monday morning at the Police Station and I asked him how they had resolved the suicide situation. He told me how they had talked him into surrendering and concluded by saying, "You are lucky you didn't go in there."

I asked why, and he told me that the male said he planned to kill me in revenge for his mate's suicide. He was sitting on the floor in a bedroom at the end of the hallway and planned to give me one barrel of the shotgun and kill himself with the second when I walked in. He reasoned that my sister caused his mate to kill himself, so he would take his revenge out on me before killing himself.

The desire to get even for a perceived wrong is one of the five instigators for anger, and anger leads to aggression. This was a glaring example of how a person can be motivated by revenge to kill someone that has no direct responsibility for their anger.

This was the first time that someone desire to kill themselves put me in danger. The second came only four months later.

IT IS GOING TO HAPPEN QUICKLY

It's a difficult line to tread, where in the blink of an eye you jump from saving someone's life to saving your own.

— Author

At 2130 hours on Monday, 30th May 1988, I was off-duty and recalled to attend a 'shots fired' situation at Hillwood on the East Tamar south of George Town. Uniform officers were in attendance and had contacted Inspector Jimmy Jones, who requested my presence.

Hillwood is a small rural town, more a hamlet, about 25 kilometers from Launceston. It is located on the East Tamar River and its population back then was probably less than one hundred people. The incident scene was on a road that ran along the riverbank with no lighting and no nearby houses. It was a very dark, secluded place. The subject's vehicle was parked just off the left side of the road adjacent to a grass paddock, and he was sitting in the driver's seat when I arrived.

I parked well back from the scene and approached Sergeant Ted George standing on the roadside. He told me that the subject was armed with a .30 caliber M1 carbine and wanted to shoot himself.

Apparently, he had fired a few shots off, which had led to the police being called. I was told that Senior Constable David Gibson had been sitting in the car negotiating with the subject for some time and was getting nowhere with him. I asked David questions about the person's attitude and he told me he seemed determined to kill himself but was calm now.

I was quite surprised that David had been sitting in the car with him because that is something I wouldn't do. Apart from the risk of the bloke deciding to take you out with him, there is also the risk of him blowing his head off and killing you at the same time.

At close range, a bone fragment can be as fatal as a ricocheting bullet.

A high-powered rifle bullet to the head sends bone and brain matter flying like shrapnel. The bullet's velocity is bad enough, but at real close range, it is made worse by the force of the gasses behind the bullet. Who wants to be splattered by blood, brain, and bone? I had been splattered by blood and brain matter once before, although, under different circumstances, it isn't pleasant!

I had also seen the damage bone fragments could do when I attended a suicide in 1977, where an elderly man had blown his head off with a 12-gauge shotgun at the front door of his house.

Pieces of his skull were sticking out of the ceiling in the hallway and lounge room. Blood and brain matter were sprayed on the ceiling, floor, and walls all the way down the hall. The top of his scalp was ten meters away on the kitchen floor. There is no way I want to be within a bull's roar of someone blowing their head off.

Through studying law enforcement tactics, I learned to approach people threatening suicide with great caution because a lot could go wrong very quickly. My experience four months before was the "I told you so" moment to make me take it seriously and recognize the risks involved.

Any situation involving an angry person with a firearm caused me to feel a substantial degree of fear. Obviously, there is the risk of being killed deliberately or as collateral damage. That is one aspect. But for me, there was the more dominant fear of failure or lack of courage to do what was necessary to control a situation. I feel a bit of pride that I stopped people from killing themselves.

Before I got wiser through experience, I would approach these jobs with the primary aim of saving a life. In the end, I approached them with the attitude of staying alive first and doing my best to stop a person killing themselves was the lessor priority. If the person was determined to take their life, so be it.

Don't misunderstand me about this, though. My approach was always calculated to do the best I could to achieve both objectives, but I was not reckless about it. I describe it like this: it is like sliding your fingers along the edge of a razor blade without cutting yourself. If you push too hard, you will get cut, and if you don't push at all, you aren't trying hard enough.

Back to the story. Inspector Jimmy Jones pulled up behind the subject's vehicle, where I was talking to David. His car headlights lit up the scene for the first time since I arrived.

It was time for me to get involved. I had all the background information that was immediately available and I understood the lay of the land.

I approached the driver's side rear passenger door from the middle of the road and saw the subject sitting in the driver's seat. As I got within a few meters, I quietly spoke to the subject, not wanting to startle him and not wanting to walk into a bullet. "G'day mate, I am Detective Sergeant Dyson. Can we have a chat and see what we can do to help you?"

I can't remember the exact words he used, but it was to the effect, "fuck off and leave me alone. It's nothing to do with the cops."

Using all the typical calming type of words used by cops in these situations, I walked up to the rear door on the driver's side of the car. "You could be right, but let's not rush into anything just yet," I said. "Maybe we can help you out with whatever the problem is. Let's just talk things over for a few minutes".

The lights from the Inspector's car cast the interior of the subject's car into shadowed darkness. This is what I thought I saw.

The man was staring straight ahead. His window was wound down halfway. The butt of the rifle was on his lap, and I thought the barrel was pointed outward towards the passenger's side of the car. I thought I was safe standing beside the rear passenger's door. My position there meant that the man had to turn his head towards me to speak to me. I asked him to step out of the car, so we could "talk this through without anyone getting hurt." Again, he told me to fuck off and leave him alone. His voice was 'deadly' calm and he kept staring straight ahead. That was a warning sign that the fellow was not going to be talked out of this quickly.

My gut instinct started warning me that there was something about this situation that reeked of danger. I could smell it in the air, my inner red flags were waving, and I felt apprehensive fear of what might happen next.

My knees started to shake and my shoulders were tense. My breathing was starting to go shallow, so I took a couple of quiet deep breaths. "What if he suddenly leaps from the car" was one possibility, and "what if he pulls the trigger while I am standing so close," was another.

I softened my tone of voice hoping to keep him calm. No pleading or begging, though. I needed to give him confidence that I was not there to cause him any trouble. I did not get close to the first base, though, because this bloke was determined to kill himself.

Within a few minutes, he said something like, "Fuck this, I've had enough." He reached down beside the driver's door. I thought he was going to wind his window up. Then I heard the blood-chilling sound of a rifle bolt chambering a round. His movement enable me to see through the shadows that he already had the rifle barrel under his chin.

The butt was between his knees, and he was reaching for the trigger.

The barrel was pointed under his chin at an angle that was also aimed at me.

My head was next to the door pillar, about 500 mm from his head. If he pulled the trigger in that instant, I was a dead man.

This all happened in the blink of an eye! The next few seconds came to me in slow motion. My movements felt like lead weights were slowing me down. I expected to hear the gunshot as I started to move, and in my mind, I could feel where the bullet was going to hit me in the back of the head as I turned away from the barrel.

I ducked my head out of the path of the bullet that I thought was about to come my way. I was trying to protect my face from the bullet, bone, and glass fragments.

I swung away from the trajectory, I anticipated that the bullet would travel through his head and yelled, "No!" I yelled at the top of my voice.

What happened next was nothing short of hilarious (in hindsight). It was like I had thrown a cat into a flock of pigeons.

I ran towards the back of his car and ducked down behind the trunk. At this same moment, a whole heap of things happened. One of the officers bolted for the paddock and got tangled in the top wires of the barbed wire fence as he jumped over it. He was snagged and trying to pull himself free like a rabbit caught in a snare.

Another officer ran down the road past the Inspector's car like the devil himself was on his tail. I imagine he was saying to himself, "Lord, oh lord, lend wings to my heels."

The Inspector floored the accelerator in his car and took off down the road in reverse gear with tires smoking as they screamed on the asphalt. He didn't care what was behind him as long as there was distance in front.

I reckon that Jimmy would still be in reverse gear somewhere out in the middle of Bass Strait if the brakes had failed! I still laugh about the visual memory of all the commotion I caused.

It is incredible how the human brain can process a lot of information in a moment of crisis.

My senses switched from the visual focus as soon as I knew I was out of the firing line. I then relied on sound and my hearing to follow what he was doing.

A gunshot would mean he was dead, and the car door opening would indicate that the situation was about to get a whole lot worse because he could come gunning for us.

Therefore, the second scenario became my priority, and where everyone was positioned became my focus. I reckon that is why I can clearly remember what everyone did in that split second or two.

No shot was fired!

Damn, I thought, he isn't dead, and he did not get out of the car, so I had to get back into the game immediately before something bad happened!

I ran crouched to the other side of the road opposite the subject's car to find some cover in the darkness. The Inspector's lights still lit up the scene from a distance. I waited for a moment to observe the driver and work out another plan of attack.

Suddenly the bloke opened his car door and started to step out. His right hand was empty. I had assumed he was right-handed, so I thought he was getting out unarmed. Great! It looked like he was giving up.

Expecting him to surrender, I stepped out onto the middle of the road, approximately 3 meters from him. Wrong move!!

He was left-handed.

The moment he was on two feet, he raised the rifle in front of him, stood crouched, and pointed the rifle right at my chest, saying, "You want in on this. You're coming too then!"

I was in a bad spot.

He was crouched, his face was black and aggressive, and his tone sounded as though he was resolved to kill. He had a strong grip on the rifle and I was momentarily stunned.

I remember thinking, "You fucking idiot Michael, now look what you've got yourself into." I had not expected this.

I was right up shit creek without a paddle. I had to think fast because a bullet with my name on it was just a finger twitch away. Twice in less than two minutes, I am facing a fucking bullet – how many more ways could I fuck this situation up by misreading the situation.

I was cold-decked, and once again, I felt my old friend fear going to work on my chest and arms.

Having a firearm pointed at you is not to be taken lightly, ever!

My body tensed all over and it felt that I was trying to make myself thinner and a smaller target. My brain was going at a million miles an hour as I weighed up my options. I was armed, but I did not think I could outdraw him. I couldn't out-run a bullet and running might cause him to shoot anyway.

I saw his finger on the trigger and knew that I couldn't do anything fast enough to stop him from pulling it. I could see the anger on his face and felt that I was a moment away from having my guts blown out my back.

The 9mm Browning semi-automatic pistol I carried was safe and securely fastened in its holster on my hip. It was as useless as an ashtray on a motor cycle.

There was no way I could have sidestepped far and fast enough to avoid his shot and draw my pistol before he shot me in the chest. Getting into a gunfight with this bloke was not an option.

The M1 carbine was pointed at my chest and his finger was on the trigger. I couldn't close the distance between him and me to deflect the barrel before he put a bullet in my chest.

I had no cover between him and me and no cover behind me for at least 10 meters.

I had used a .30 caliber carbine to shoot wallaby. I had seen the damage it caused - a small entry wound and blood and guts out the exit wound. Those images flashed through my mind in an instant.

My chest felt as though it was tightening as my breathing became shallow. Adrenalin flooded my body. I forced myself to breathe slowly and deeply to reduce the tension. I had to think and do something, but what? One wrong move and I was dead with my guts blown out my back.

All that mattered to me was my own survival.

My vision was very focused, almost tunnel vision: I could see his finger on the trigger. The only time I looked at the barrel was in the first instant, enough for me to know that he was on target.

The rifle was no longer relevant to my survival because I couldn't do anything about getting out of the line of fire. The man had to be my only focus because he controlled the rifle. I couldn't physically control him, so all I had left were my persuasion skills.

Everyone has heard the term fight or flight, but there is a third option; freeze. Those first two options were gone, so I had one option left. Freeze.

I needed to talk and personalize with him – fast! I had eye-to-eye contact with him, which was in my favor, so I took advantage of it.

I focused on his eyes like I was looking into his skull. I wanted to penetrate the fog in his head. I needed to know that he was listening to me, and most importantly, hearing me. I needed to see that he was paying attention. I was not aware of anything else around me.

I had no idea where the other officers were by now or what they were doing. It was just me and the subject. The only sound I was tuned into was his voice – I don't remember hearing mine. I am still conscious of observing his shoulders in the periphery; I needed to see any tensing or relaxing. If he tensed, I was dead, if he relaxed, I might have an opportunity to get out of the line of fire.

I raised both my hands in surrender to reduce any perception of threat. To make myself as non-threatening as possible, I said, "There is no need to shoot me.

I will not stop you from killing yourself if that's what you want, so there is no need to kill me." I was pleading for my life.

He stayed silent, crouching forward aggressively, looking straight at me, finger on the trigger. But I could see the fire slowly going out of his eyes. It looked like he was thinking!

I did not stop talking; words rolled off my tongue like this was my only chance to avoid getting shot.

I told him that I could understand why he felt the need to kill himself, but I did not want to die yet. I told him that I had a wife and kids to go home to, and they needed me alive. I told him that I only wanted to save his life, but if he wanted to die that badly, go ahead, but don't kill me.

I saw his shoulders relax slightly. I was making progress. I kept talking. I told him he was free to leave. Then he lowered the rifle as the tension went out of his shoulders. He said, "I don't need to kill you." Then he walked to the back of the car, urinated, got back into the car, and drove off.

It was too dangerous to chase after him immediately, so we let him go to give him some space.

I recall visiting a house that night – it might have been to speak to his wife or find out if he had returned home. I believe the bloke shot himself somewhere else; if not that night, it was later on. I have never worried about that, though; there was nothing more I could have done to stop it. I do not stress about the bad outcomes provided that I am satisfied that I did the best I could at the time.

The entire situation took 4 hours to resolve, which equates to 4 hours of tense and stressful decision making.

I stuffed up tactically this time. I was over-confident. I thought that I was a good negotiator and I was too confident that I could talk him down. I forgot that a person wanting to commit suicide could become a threat to someone else. I debriefed myself over the next few days. I kicked myself for having walked into an armed encounter with a holstered pistol.

I was a finger twitch away from getting killed, and I was scared. There was no way I would admit that to my colleagues, though; I wanted them to think that I carried it all off as though it was nothing out of the ordinary.

I went home and lay in bed, thinking that I shouldn't have been as scared as I genuinely felt.

I still had the mindset that real men don't get scared; they take action. This was the closest I had come to being killed, and I felt like a coward, mostly because when I screamed "no," I was genuinely scared.

I started second-guessing myself. Did I have the guts to take on the genuinely hard jobs in the future. The type of jobs where you had to walk onto the two-way range when the bullets were flying.

I did not want to talk to anyone about it. It was all in a day's work, but I knew I was deceiving myself because I knew how much that situation scared me. If I told anyone how I really felt, they would have thought I was weak as piss and not be confident in me in the future.

But there was an awakening in me that night. It came to me like something out of the dark; a calm resolve. A cold, hard, relaxed feeling came from deep inside me. I realized that I would kill to save my life or the life of someone else.

I was aware that I could get into worse situations, and I had to do something to make sure I was up to the job. At that time, I was still new in the Special Operations Group, and there was no way I could be afraid of being at the pointy end of a gun on the two-way rifle range.

All the SOG training involved teamwork, which means you are fully backed up in a firefight, but it's different when you are on your own.

I made two significant decisions as a result of this experience. One was that I would never, ever let anyone point a gun at me again, and the second was that it would be better to be tried by 12 than carried by 6.

I became more determined to fix that with physical training to become stronger, faster, and more skilled with a firearm. I got very serious about learning everything I could about human aggression, defensive and offensive tactics, and the law. It was around this time that my interest in the theory of crisis decision making became aroused.

ATTACK IS THE SECRET OF DEFENCE

Trying to understand the behavior of some people is like trying to smell the color 9.

— Unknown

There was always a lot going on in George Town in the four years I was posted there. Our CIB branch covered the north-east of Tasmania, which was the largest geographic district in the State. When I started there, it was covered by two investigators, and later, a third joined the team.

Young violent men in the town seemed to be competing to see who was the bravest and most violent criminal on the patch. It was the most violent and potentially dangerous place I had worked.

In April and May 1987, our work included searching remote properties for an armed offender, investigating the shooting of a young man with a shotgun, and the attempted rape of a young woman. I worked over 72 hours of overtime in those two months.

A suspect for several crimes, including sexual assault, attempted to set up an ambush to assassinate my partner and me at this time. His nickname was Snowy.

Snowy, a reputed violent criminal and a drug addict, got out of prison a few months before, and the town was in fear of his return.

Hotels hired security guards and guard dogs because, in the past, he had threatened to attack one hotel with a chainsaw. It is fair to say that the general duties police were also afraid of his return to town. I was in the process of being promoted to Detective Sergeant and was, therefore, ultimately responsible for handling this problem.

As soon as he arrived in town, I confronted Snowy on the street and identified myself. He spoke the words of a reformed criminal, saying that he was going straight and had no intention of getting into trouble.

He was taking me for a fool. I could tell by the sinister look in his eyes as he spoke that he was insolent and trying to intimidate me. I was not going to take any shit from him and needed him to know it.

I told him that he was welcome back in town, provided he obeyed the law. However, I told him that if he committed any crime or caused any trouble, I would be over his arse like a nappy rash, and I wouldn't be gentle about it. "Sure, Sergeant, I am not going to be any problem at all," he said with a smug look on his face.

Honestly, I felt excited about the challenge. Snowy knew people were afraid of him, and he loved his notoriety. He would terrorize the town like he was Al Capone, but I had made up my mind to stop him at any cost.

If he screwed up, I was going to tear him to shreds so badly that he would never want to get on the wrong side of the law again. Under no circumstances was I going to let him intimidate the police or the citizens.

In no time, the burglary rate started going up, and cars were being stolen, which were crimes that fitted the Snowy's form.

He had a mad mate who got the nickname Screwnut because of his ugly head and protruding ears. Screwnut looked like a clown without a hat. He was a character and a prolific small-time crook searching for the big time in the town.

We arrested Screwnut once for a burglary, where he dropped his bank book outside the window where he broke into a building. He was the dumbest crook I ever met and one of the first I met when I arrived in town.

The uniform cops said that Screwnut was spreading the word around town that he would take me, "the new cop," on. They told me Screwnut was just a simple fool, but I should be careful of him. I asked them to let me know when they caught up with him, and I would introduce myself to him.

Soon after, I saw Screwnut walking past the police station. I caught up with him outside and, after a brief introduction, I invited Screwnut into the station cellblock exercise yard for a private talk between him and me.

He came along with me, and in the yard, I told him that I heard that he wanted to have a crack at me, and I offered him the chance there and then to have a go.

I got a nice spontaneous apology from him, and he promised that he would not threaten me again. That didn't last long, though.

However, when Screwnut joined up with Snowy, there was a potentially volatile and unpredictable mix of lunacy, drug-influenced violence, and that is how it turned out. Snowy was the 'brains' of the outfit and by far the most dangerous, so I was told.

I think the assault of the young woman was around the same time that Snowy stole one of the local fire brigade vehicles because I charged him with both crimes simultaneously. He had gone right off the rails.

It took me a few weeks to run Snowy to ground before I arrested him on May 26th. This is how it went down.

I received information from a couple of sources within his cohort that Snowy had armed himself and prepared to shoot it out.

My partner and I started engaging with informants and visiting known associates. The information about him being armed was credible and from multiple sources. Therefore, we took no chances and used tactical entries at every house we searched. I would leave each householder with the warning that if they harbored Snowy, we would be back and keep on kicking doors in until he was under arrest.

At 1500 hours on Saturday, 16th May, I was called in from a day off because Snowy and Screwnut were seen in a local park. When we arrived, they ran into the bush. We searched for them, of course, but couldn't locate them.

At 1900 hours, I received a telephone call at home from Screwnut. He said that Snowy wanted to meet me on my own at a nearby railway siding.

Shortly after that, Snowy called me on the phone, saying that he was going to kill me when he caught up with me. I told him that he would have that opportunity because I would be at the railway siding waiting for him at the appointed time of 2300 hours that night.

I was at the railway siding at 2230 hours and stayed there until 2330. Snowy did not turn up.

After I got home, I hadn't long been in bed when the telephone rang. When I answered, I heard, "Is that you Dyson?"

"Who's this?" I asked.

"It's Snowy, you cunt, and I am coming after you."

I deliberately and calmly replied "Where the fuck are you, you little prick? I'll make it easy for you. Tell me where you are, and I'll be there straight away."

He shouted, "I am going to get you, you cunt, you've been harassing my friends, and you're going to pay."

In a slightly firmer tone I said, "I am going to tear this town apart until I've got you, you son of a bitch. Tell me where you are and give yourself up if you are so worried about your *fucking* mates."

His tone went up to the point where he was shouting at hysterically.

"No," he screamed, "I am coming after you, and I am going to blow you away, you lousy cunt."

I sat up on the edge of the bed and roared "Fuck you!! Tell me where you are you gutless piece of shit, and I will come to you right now."

You are mistaken if you think I was losing control of myself. On the contrary, this was a battle of wills and I was escalating my tone to dominate Snowy's will.

The more I dominated his tone and demanded to see him straight away, the lower his tone became until he was sort of whimpering, "No - it's me coming after you."

In the end, I finished the now pointless conversation by saying that I would run him down eventually, and I slammed the phone back down on the receiver. I wanted him to think that I was one hell of a dangerous son of a bitch.

I was fired up. Snowy was openly threatening to kill me! I was more offended by that than anything else. As tense as this situation had become, I would be lying if I said that I wasn't excited about the challenge.

There I sat. Sitting on the edge of the bed thinking about who knows what when I heard some sobbing beside me. I looked at my wife and saw she was crying. When I asked her what was wrong, she replied, "I didn't know you were so violent."

I never discussed too much about work with my wife, especially not the dangerous side of the job. This time I had just inadvertently brought it home.

The trouble was that she saw me as the violent one, not knowing what I was dealing with at the other end of the phone. I did not tell her anything about Snowy threatening to kill me or anything else about the case. It would only have frightened her more – better the devil she knew, I guess.

The next morning when I arrived at work, I took a phone call from one of my best informants, one of the gang leaders that Snowy was mixed up with. This informant ran with the fox and hunted with the hounds. She was a criminal but traded off favors (No – not those sort of favors) by giving me information about the more serious stuff that was going on.

I could tell that the informant was concerned. She told me that I had to be careful because Snowy and Screwnut were serious about killing me. She told me the telephone call last night was made from her house.

She said that after I had hung up on Snowy, he asked her to call me back to tell me that he was at her house. She lived towards the end of a cul-de-sac, and Snowy planned to be waiting under some shrubs when I arrived. He had a double-barrel shotgun; and the plan was to kill my partner and me before we could get out of the car.

The informant wanted no part of it and refused. She said Screwnut and Snowy left not long after arguing with her about setting up the shooting.

That was credible information that made me concerned about being ambushed. Not only was I in danger, so was my partner. It could happen any day at any place. My senses were on a very high level of alert 24/7 at this time.

I changed from the day shift to the afternoon shift after the day after that call. I was going to tear the town to pieces to find Snowy.

I visited the local Justice of the Peace and swore out a warrant for his arrest. The warrant gave me the power to use all reasonable force to enter any property where I had reason to believe he could be located. The repeated threats to kill me gave me justification to hit those places hard and by surprise.

Once I had the warrant, I met with several informants who gave me additional information about where I might find Snowy.

I prioritized my targets and developed a plan of attack. Then I pulled together a team of my partner and two uniform officers. I briefed them at the police station on what was going on and the procedures we were going to follow and the tactics we were going to use. That night we searched nine premises and patrolled the streets looking for Snowy.

Our house entry procedures were simple. *Knock fucking knock!*

We entered each house by surprise. The only knocking the occupants heard was us kicking in the doors. We used aggressive room clearance tactics for shock value intended to deter any resistance or threat from the occupants.

We put the cat among the pigeons because I told every known associate that I would not stop searching their houses until Snowy was found and in custody.

These searches went on for the next four days. They had the desired effect because they were limiting the places that Snowy could hide. Many of his associates did not want him around them in fear of a return visit from the police.

The breakthrough came on day seven when, at about midday, a call was received at the station to tell us where Snowy was right at that moment. I gathered every on-duty officer at the station, about five of them, and gave them a quick briefing.

Two uniform officers, one of them would go to the front door to make the announcement, and one would stand back on the street in case Snowy tried to escape through a window. One other would approach with me from the rear over a back fence that bordered vacant land, which was Snowy's most likely escape route. I wanted to meet him head-on.

Our timing was perfect. Just as I vaulted the back fence, I saw Snowy bolting towards me out the back door of the house. By the time he was able to stop and turn around, I had hit the ground running and was about 10 yards behind him.

He crashed through the back door, and I had closed to about 5 yards behind him. He ran down the hall of the house, which led to the front door. I saw the two uniformed officers at the front door talking to the lady of the house. Snowy ran left into a front room, and I was only a few yards behind him.

I was able to follow his movement visually and by sound. The door was hinged on the right side as I faced it. As he went into the room, it swung back half shut. I heard him move behind the door and saw through the crack in the door that he had grabbed something from behind the door that looked like a shotgun barrel.

I did not break stride; I hit the door with my shoulder with all the force I could and entered the room in a standard CQB (close-quarter-battle) move. I was only focused on Snowy's face, and I had my .38 snub-nosed revolver cocked and aimed between his eyes at less than two meters. I shouted as aggressively (no, violently) as I could, "Drop it, or I *will* blow your *fucking* head off."

Although I was totally focused on his face, I could see that he held what could have been a shotgun. The barrel was not aimed at me, but it wasn't going to take much of a movement to change that. If he moved it towards me, he was dead.

The woman was screaming hysterically, "No, not in my house, no!"

Where the fuck was Screwnut? I could almost feel the bullet in my back – I had to end this fast.

I was conscious of the risk of me being attacked from behind. I was the only tactical officer on the team and could only hope that the other officers had my back covered. They arrived within seconds.

I took one pace forward, and I almost had the barrel of the pistol on Snowy's forehead. "Drop it now!" I shouted.

I needed as much shock value out of my actions as I could muster. Snowy dropped the broom he was holding and thrust his arms in the air. "Don't shoot, don't shoot, I give up," he shouted.

A fucking broom! He was holding a fucking broom against an armed and aggressive police officer that he had threatened to kill with a shotgun! Criminals are so dumb, and it is no wonder people find it difficult to believe 'suicide by cop' is a real thing.

"Turn around!" I ordered.

Snowy was totally compliant and non-resistant. I placed him under arrest in the normal way and handcuffed him.

I mustered him to the front door where the woman was leaning against the wall sobbing. I saw other people in the living room as I passed the door, but had no idea who they were, but they were immobile in their chairs. I put him in the back of the police car and got into the back seat with him; the driver was my partner.

I had a little chat with Snowy about threatening to kill me on the 10-minute drive back to the station. By the time we arrived, he was sobbing like a child.

I put him through the charging procedure locked him in a cell. I think he was remanded in custody, pleaded guilty in court at a later date, and served a short prison sentence.

Snowy never returned to George Town after his release, but it was not the last time I dealt with him.

The last time I dealt with Snowy was after his release from prison in November. He had moved into a town 70 kilometers from George Town.

On the 6th of November, I was sitting in the muster room at the police station in George Town when I heard a call over the radio that Snowy had stolen a car and was on the Bridport Highway traveling towards George Town.

We had just taken delivery of a brand new V6 Commodore police car. This was the fastest vehicle I had driven and here was a chance to test it out in a car chase. We headed out of town towards the junction of the East Tamar Highway and Bridport Road. The junction is at the end of a long straight stretch of road and it is big because of heavy transport use.

The engine governor was pinging out as I approached the intersection. That means I was at top speed, which from memory was around 200 km/hour.

As I turned into Bridport Road I didn't allow for the loose blue metal that was off the driving line in the junction. The car went into a slide onto the opposite side of the road and was heading for the trees. My partner was hanging on and sort of screaming at the same time.

I got the thing under control and straightened up heading east. I adjusted myself in my seat, took a breath, and looked over at my partner with a bit of a grin on my face. "Fuck me, mate. She handles well in a slide," I said. I could tell by the look on his face that it didn't impress him much. It was going to take a minute or two for me to stop shaking though. That was a near miss that frightened the shit out of me.

The Bridport Road was a beautiful thing. It had a great surface, long straights, and racy high-speed corners. I kept the engine governor pinging all the way until we came across Snowy heading west.

I saw him coming from the other end of a short straight. I stood on the brakes and put the ABS braking system to the test. The wheels didn't lock up, but there we created a big cloud of tire smoke.

I had almost got the car pulled up as Snowy roared past us. I did a U-turn and was almost back up to maximum speed when I saw dust rising in the distance. I said to my partner, "Fuck it. Don't tell me he has crashed already; we haven't even started."

I was looking forward to the chase because Snowy also had a reputation as a runner when he stole a car.

We drove onto the stolen vehicle, which he had plowed into a steep embankment on the left side of the road. He hadn't crashed it but had put it into the bank. I pulled up and told my partner to take the keys out of the ignition – I was going to chase him on foot.

Snowy had been an excellent athlete, especially at middle distance running, but I had also been a middle-distance runner. I was very fit and knew that I could outlast him even if we had to run all the way to George Town. Up the embankment, I ran and jumped the wire fence at the top.

There was a sandy track that ran parallel to the road, and I could see his footprints in the sand. It was a forested area with plenty of concealment for him, so I put my pistol in my hand and set off at a jog along the track.

I hadn't run 100 yards before Snowy appeared from behind a large tree on the right side of the track with his hands in the air.

He said, "I am sorry, Mr. Dyson, I didn't know it was you," and he meekly walked towards me and surrendered. Our return trip to George Town was quite sociable and friendly, we even had a laugh together. Snowy was never going to be a threat to me again.

You might ask where the fear in this story was, well let me tell you, it is all through it. The fear built up over those weeks as the threat to my life was confirmed and became imminent.

My partner and I could have been killed anywhere at any time – I even carried my revolver when I played golf. All it needed was for them to take enough drugs and talk themselves into it.

My vigilance of my surroundings was very high – as high as I knew how to make it. I went to the local pistol range almost daily. I practiced fast draw and accuracy with the snub-nosed revolver (I was still not allowed to carry the 9mm on general duties).

I am sure that my partners at the time would confirm how good I became with the .38 revolver – as far as I was concerned, my life depended on it. I was totally confident of a headshot at ten yards, a moving body shot at the same distance, and an elbow or shoulder shot at five yards static.

I ran every day and worked out on weights in the evening. As I trained, I imagined the strength I would need to have to break bones in a life and death fight. I trained to break a man's arm, neck, or back.

On the pistol range and while working out, I ran scenario after scenario in my mind of how I could be attacked and how I could respond. I mentally practiced and rehearsed what I would do to overcome whatever they threw at me.

When the time came to arrest Snowy, the fear had developed into controlled aggression. I was ready physically and mentally to kill him if the need arose – no hesitation.

How do I relate that preparation to the reality of what happened? I did not over-react to what I thought was the shotgun in his hands, nor did I hesitate to confront the threat and carry out my duty.

Snowy was lucky that day.

TRAIN TO PREPARE AGAINST SURPRISE

*It is incredible how quickly things can turn around when you are deal-
ing with crazy people.*

I worked the CIB duty car afternoon shift with a newly sworn Constable on
Saturday, 16th March 1991. At 2115 hours, we received a report of a trespasser at
a hotel. We were given sketchy details about someone refusing to leave licensed
premises, which could have been a simple drunk being refused service in the
bottle shop.

It turned out to be a minor domestic argument over a $40 black and white portable
TV. It ended up in a violent encounter that shocked the young Constable to his core.

We parked our car on the street beside the bottle shop. Everything was quiet.
I noticed an old car occupied by two males and a large dog parked in the bottle
shop driveway.

I did not know at that stage that those people were the source of the problem.

We walked behind the car σ into the bottle shop to meet the owner. The
driver was arguing with a woman over a TV set and refused to leave until she gave
it to him. He had been a pest in previous days by standing outside and shouting
abuse and obscenities at the female who lived on the hotel's first floor.

This time he was refusing to move his vehicle until the female gave him the
TV. The hotel owner had told the driver that he was not permitted on the premises and said to me that he wanted the driver and vehicle moved on.

Looking through the doorway, I saw that the driver was a middle-aged man
and his passenger appeared to be in his 20's. Both were sitting calmly in the car
but were staring straight ahead, like a thousand-yard stare.

They were too calm under the circumstances for my comfort. It gave me a
warning of potential trouble to come.

They gave the impression that they were ignoring our presence. Something
like, "Police? What police? Nothing to do with us." It was not normal behavior for

this type of situation. A normal person would get out of the car and try to justify themselves. The alternatives would be to drive off to avoid a confrontation with the police or go on the attack.

My next step was to speak to the woman involved. Before I talked to the driver, I needed some background information to avoid a confrontation, like a lengthy argument about who was right or wrong.

If I simply did as the hotel owner asked and tried to move them on, I was likely to get an argument and all sorts of stories from the two men. I decided to play dumb with the occupants of the car to avoid a confrontation. I would wait until I had more information before I tackled them.

I walked past the car as though I had no interest in it or its occupants.

Upstairs in her room, the woman told me that she had been in an on-again-off-again relationship with the older male driving the car downstairs. When she was short of cash, he would offer to help her out, not a loan, but a gift. However, when he ran short of cash, he would harass her and forcibly take back what he had given her to feed his gambling habit.

She said that she had several restraint orders made against him in the past and had another one issued but not served on him. She had been evicted from other places she lived because the male would upset her neighbors by causing trouble for her through his abusive behavior.

She said that she was terrified of the male's son, the passenger in the car, because he was very violent and would do anything for his father. She claimed that she had paid for the television, and she would not let him have it under any circumstances.

I suggested that she have the restraint order served and do nothing to provoke him to violence, which included accepting any more money or gifts from him. She agreed to that.

My assessment was something like this. Two males who had known violent behavior in the past. Both exhibiting signs of belligerence and non-compliant behavior. They had come prepared for a stand-off with the woman and were not concerned about involving others in the situation. They weren't worried about being told to leave by the property owner; they were prepared to sit it out knowing that the police were being called. The dog was an unknown factor; it could be vicious or not.

The threats that I anticipated coming from this situation were: an argument about who was right or wrong; refusing to leave forcing me to make an arrest, leading to a violent arrest; man, youth and dog becoming violent and attacking my partner and me to avoid arrest, or both males ignoring me forcing me to break into the car to make an arrest.

The only way forward was to make contact and negotiate with the driver and take the rest as it came along.

But there had to be no-nonsense in my approach, nor any sign of uncertainty. If I showed any lack of resolve or confidence, the culprits would take the high ground, and we would get nowhere. This was a boring call, and I was not in the mood for playing stupid games. This was not going to take long as far as I was concerned.

I went through my options as I walked down the external stairs to the driveway.

I was covered by the Criminal Code to use reasonable force to remove a trespasser or disorderly person from the property. The owner of the hotel had asked them to leave, and our job was to ensure they left. That was the baseline from which I was not going to budge. If they escalated it beyond that, the problem would be theirs.

I was very confident in my physical ability to deal with both males simultaneously if necessary. It wouldn't be pretty and it could be extremely violent.

If the dog got involved, we would have to disable the men quickly, so the dog could be shot before it savaged either of us. The men would have to come first and the dog second. Despite having confidence in my plan, I enjoyed the feeling of fear of the unknown building up in me.

By this point in my career, I had come to welcome the adrenaline rush. I knew my mind was alert, and my body was ready for action, and I knew what I could and could not do in response to any of the scenarios I had rehearsed in my mind.

Domestic disputes are dangerous and should have a fear factor around them. They are unpredictable, dynamic, and can turn violent in an instant.

I can understand someone questioning what made me feel afraid when this appears to be a routine domestic dispute call.

There are two immediate answers: one, there is no such thing as a routine domestic dispute call. Domestic violence calls are potentially dangerous for law enforcement, and second, was the man's thousand-yard stare. Anything could happen.

The thousand-yard stare is a phrase coined to describe the limp unfocused gaze of a battle-weary soldier. It is a characteristic of post-traumatic stress disorder where the despondent stare reflects dissociation from trauma.

A cognitive aggressor exhibits a dissociation from the victim/s and/or the act they are about to commit. The aggressor displays a cold, calculating, calm appearance, unlike the primal aggressor who exhibits a red-faced, ready to explode attitude.

On the way down the stairs, I had time to give the Constable a quick briefing and outline my plan of attack. It was not much more than, "We are going to remove these people as trespassers. We have all the power and authority we need to do that, but this could get ugly, so be ready for anything. Let me do the talking, and you stand back a couple of meters to watch my back. If the passenger gets out of the car, you deal with him and keep him off my back." The young fellow was good to go.

The driver had his window down, and as I approached him, he said, "I am not moving from here until I get my TV back," and he locked the driver's side door. I hadn't said a word and he was staring fixedly ahead, not making eye contact.

I said, "I am Detective Sergeant Dyson from the Hobart CIB. Unlock the door and get out of the car. I want to talk to you, so we can sort something out". He said, "I am not moving from here!" and told his son, "Lock your door, don't let them in." His cold calm voice and thousand-yard stare took me up to red-alert. Trouble was brewing, of that, I had no doubt.

He said he owed someone $40 for the television, and he was not going anywhere until he got it. In these few sentences, his tone escalated from calm to belligerent.

I told him to see a solicitor if he had a claim, but he had trouble with the police right now. He said he had done nothing wrong and for us to leave him alone. I explained that he had no right to block the hotel driveway and he was trespassing if he did not move on.

I wondered if the driver could be intoxicated or under the influence of a drug, so I asked him if he had been drinking. He snarled a reply that he hadn't had a drink for six years, and that was why he wouldn't go into the hotel to get the television himself. The question of drugs mixed with his body language, tone of voice, and alleged propensity to violence made this a dangerous encounter.

I told him to get out of the car, and he reached forward, turned on the ignition, and started the car. I told him that I would not allow him to drive the car until he had taken a breath test. He paid no notice of me and started to drive off.

I put my hand on the windshield in front of him and said, "This is not going to do you any good. I will chase you all over Hobart if necessary until you stop, now turn the car off!"

He turned off the ignition, but his physical signs changed as he did that. His shoulders hunched upwards; he took a deep breath, and his arms and hands tensed on the steering wheel. He was about to explode. I said, "Don't do anything stupid. Come on, get out of the car and let's get this sorted out; it won't take long." He looked like he was wound up as tight as a fiddle string, and he said flatly, "I am not going anywhere!"

Suddenly he lunged towards the floor near the feet of his passenger. I had no idea what he was reaching for, except it was more likely to be a weapon than a sandwich, so I stepped one pace back and to the side to place myself just behind his right shoulder.

At the same time, I executed what I reckon might be the fastest draw of my pistol ever. I brought it up to a two-handed grip and, at the ready position, pointed it at about the level of his backside.

As I reacted, I shouted, "Stop, don't move!"

Still hunched over, reaching for the floor, he looked over his shoulder and saw my pistol pointed at him. He hesitated for a nano-second and then reached towards the floor.

I raised my pistol and crouched in a close-quarter battle stance. Feet shoulder width apart, knees slightly bent, shoulders square onto the target, slightly leaning forward with my pistol aimed at his right ear. I shouted, "Don't do it! Stop! Put your hands on the steering wheel NOW!"

None of that 'freeze mother-fucker" crap you see on movies. I had stopped using that sort of language in these situations after learning that clear, precise and professional language that witnesses can remember is a defense if you are accused of being angry or out of control.

I took the first pressure on the trigger. I was as calm and cold as I had ever experienced. I was ready and willing to shoot.

I saw movement from the passenger. He was leaning forward, probably to see what I was doing. I stepped back and sideways one more pace to the right to open my line of sight in line with the door opening. I wanted to get the first glimpse of what was coming off the floor. That movement seemed to intimidate the driver a little because he sat up and put both hands on the steering wheel. Maybe he could see in my face that I was not messing around.

Plenty of people have told me that I have a cold hard looking face when I am angry. However, I was not angry. I was super-aggressive and fully committed to using deadly force, so it is only natural that I would have the countenance of a priest at a Christening.

A quick glimpse at the passenger and I saw that he was still leaning forward and appeared to be amused and enjoying the show. He posed no immediate threat, but he looked weird and worth watching out for. The driver was immobile and staring straight ahead.

The time for being nice about this had gone. I told the driver to unlock the door, or I would smash the window and pull him out of the car.

He reached over and unlocked the door. I said, "Get out of the car!" To increase my reactionary gap, I took one more step backward as he opened the door, which still did not leave much of a space between us.

His demeanor changed in the blink of an eye from non-compliant to a raving mad-man. He rushed from the car and lunged at me with a snarl on his face, and both hands raised towards my pistol; it looked like he was making a grab for it.

His empty hands attack against me, while I held my pistol on him, changed the legal situation dramatically. The encounter had changed from a potentially lethal threat to a difficult physical force situation in the blink of an eye. My pistol was now a liability.

There were three paces between us. By the time he had taken his second step, I had snapped the pistol back to the one-hand ready position above the holster on my right hip, where it was out of his reach. At the same time, I stepped forward into a martial art fighting stance to meet him halfway through his third step.

As he took the third step, his arms came into trapping range, about 50 cm from my throat. I used my left hand to catch his right arm just above his elbow. I pivoted my hips and shoulders and used his momentum to spin him around to face his car. As he tried to get his balance, I folded my left arm across his shoulders and brought my right elbow into the base of his skull as I stepped forward.

I slammed him into the side of his car so hard I thought I had broken his ribs. In that position I was able to quickly holster my pistol and pull his arms behind his back. I restrained him with my right knee slammed into the crack of his backside for added shock value, and with the Constable's help, quickly handcuffed him.

When the Constable took hold of him, I quickly re-drew my pistol and went to the front of the car to cover the passenger. I told him to get out of the car, which he did, empty-handed and making no threat. I re-holstered my pistol and met the passenger before he stood erect. I forced him to 'adopt the position' on the front of the car and frisked him – he was clean. I told him to go and stand about 10 meters away, which he did. There was no immediate sign of a threat coming from him, and he now appeared to be somewhat shocked by the suddenness of the action.

I checked the floor of the car and found that the driver was reaching for a tire lever. Not much better than a knife. These are things you shouldn't start a gunfight with.

I guess he thought he would give me a thrashing with it, or I would be intimidated into withdrawing from the situation.

The driver was still aggressive and agitated, showing signs of intoxication. He rambled about not having had a drink in six years, and he denied taking any drugs. Nonetheless, I asked the Constable to call a traffic car for a breath test.

Now the driver tried to take up the attack again, verbally this time. He rambled about police brutality and objected to having a gun pointed at him. He said if we bruised him, he would go straight to the hospital and then to a member of parliament.

The traffic car arrived and the driver was given a breath test that returned a negative reading. The traffic officer knew the driver and was able to tell me that he normally displayed the signs of drunkenness. So, we ended the situation by telling both men to clear off and keep away from the hotel, and off they went like skulking hounds.

On Monday, I arrived at work and was told by one of the Detectives that the driver had complained to the Internal Investigation Unit about me pulling a gun on him and assaulting him. An internal investigation was underway. Later, I received a copy of the claims they had made against me. When I read it, I wished I had been there to see the situation unfold as he described it. It was a good piece of fiction.

His allegations included that I was a lunatic brandishing a pistol at his head. The language he claimed I used came straight out of a Hollywood movie script. He said that I stood in front of the car with my pistol drawn and threatened to use it to stop the vehicle from driving off.

He claimed that I reached into the car to point the pistol at his son's head. That would be like handing either one or both of them my pistol.

His son claimed that I said to him, "Just stay where you are and get out of the car." How does that work? It's like yelling at a dog and telling it to get inside out. They also claimed I damaged his beat-up old car, but the details of how I was supposed to have done that are not in my notes.

The story soon got around the Detective office. One of my fellow sergeants pointed out a bulletin on the office notice board that had gone up during the week, which I hadn't seen.

I read the bulletin, and it painted a picture of a dangerous, drug-addicted man. The bulletin warned police that this person was schizophrenic, took heavy doses of valium, and was being treated by a psychologist.

A community worker who dealt with him reported that he had made open threats against his wife and threatened to kill police if they interfered. He had falsely reported to police that he and his wife had been shot at his ex-wife's address. Another call to police was to her address, claiming that the ex-husband was outside and had a gun and was going to use it.

The Detective wanted to help me justify drawing my pistol. He suggested that if I had read the bulletin, I would have all the justification I needed to draw my pistol. However, I considered it an advantage for me to admit that I had not seen the bulletin. I wanted to rely on my observations and assessment of the situation as it evolved and answer the complaint using all I knew about the lawful use of force and defensive tactics. As far as I was concerned, it was a test case.

These are the closing paragraphs of my report in response to the allegations:

Under no circumstances at any time in the future, will I allow any person to attack me or point a firearm at me. It has happened to me before on several occasions where I have been reluctant to use my weapon to protect myself. It is disconcerting to find yourself with someone pointing a firearm at you and placing themselves unlawfully in control of a situation.

That person holds the decision as to whether you live or die. I cannot allow those past situations to affect my courage to do my duty as required by law, and I much prefer to place myself in control of a situation before it is too late, because I know that no-one should get hurt if they do as they are told, which is what occurred on this occasion.

I did not place B....S or his son in jeopardy. He did that himself. It would not have happened if he was acting lawfully and had cooperated with Police.

The conclusion from the internal investigation unit was that I had acted appropriately in the circumstances. I bet it hurt them to write that up because 'internals' likes to get a kill against one of their own as much as a detective likes to catch a crook.

There is a footnote to this story, and it relates to the young Constable's experience from this event. After the situation had been resolved, we got back into the car and sat for a moment. The young fellow was not in shock, but I could tell he was affected by the events. I had been in his shoes twenty-odd years before, so I could guess what was going through his mind. Naturally, I was also concerned about how he saw things go down. He needed to be confident that all my actions were lawful and reasonable. Now was the time to talk it over, not just for a debriefing but also as a teaching and mentoring exercise.

The Constable told me that when he knocked off work that night, he would submit a report to his Inspector about what had happened. A sort of icy feeling came over me at that moment – like *what the fuck are you going to say* type of feeling that makes the old Sarge's hair stand up on the back of his neck. "What about," I asked.

He replied that the situation escalated so fast, he did not think he was equipped to deal with it. He said that if it had happened to him, he would have been fucked. He said the training in their recruit course did not go close to preparing him for what he just saw happen. He wanted to inform the Police Academy that their training was not good enough for what they could face on the street.

We spent a lot of time over the rest of the shift talking it over. I told him about how I had gotten my experience and how I had educated myself to survive on the streets. I told him to never rely on the Academy to teach you everything because that would be impossible.

I encouraged him to never stop learning from every law enforcement book he could read and every bit of experience he got. He needed to always anticipate the worst possible scenario and have a plan and the ability to carry it out.

I explained that where I went wrong was not paying closer attention to the occupants of the car when we arrived. We could have walked into an ambush and been shot in the back. However, I said that we were two steps or more ahead of a non-compliant drug-affected, violent person who knew he was heading for a confrontation with the police before we arrived. We had a plan, and we executed it perfectly. I said that he had done as I asked, and he responded just as I hoped he would when it was needed. "A job well-done mate, but make sure you learn from the experience and get better and better as you go through your career."

NEVER GIVE UP

A woman doesn't know life until she has given birth, but a man doesn't know life until he has faced death.

— Unknown

Life has a new meaning after a near-death experience. I had two of them in 1993.

I was on a diving trip on the west coast of Tasmania with a bunch of mates from the SOG. I made a couple of mistakes that almost cost me my life.

A fair bit of alcohol was drunk on the first night: correction; a bloody lot of alcohol was drunk. We were all very close mates, and we were in for a great adventure diving for crayfish.

We left Strahan in the early morning on a boat and was taken outside Hells Gates and south along the coast. A heavy two-meter swell was on the ocean, but no wind – perfect conditions.

We took it in turns to dive; my turn came last. I wanted to be close enough to shore to see the bottom before I jumped off the boat. I have a phobia about swimming in deep water. There are sharks and other things in there that want to eat me, so I have made a deal with them – if they stay out of the Cascade Hotel, I will stay out of their feeding grounds.

On this day, I spent a fair bit of time under the water exploring the bottom. I gradually got into deeper water. I was diving close to the surface when I found it difficult to breathe. I surfaced and looked to the boat, which was drifting about 50 yards away. The blokes were signaling for me to come in, and they were laughing because they had turned off the air to force me to return to the boat.

Damn it, I had to swim across deep water to the boat. It scared me, but I made it. There was no way I wanted to show the gang how scared I was of that swim.

On the way back through Hells Gates, the gearbox on one of the motors broke. After that, it was a slow trip on one engine back to port. The best way to kill time was to drink more beer.

When we got back to port in the afternoon, we bought some greasy takeaway food and drove back to Zeehan, where we were staying. On the way, someone suggested that we go skin diving in the large rock pools at Granville Harbor – a notorious piece of water. Everyone was keen, so we arrived there an hour or two before dusk.

I stayed close to shore and dived in the water, not more than one or two fathoms deep. It was late in the afternoon and getting on to twilight.

I had almost had enough and was ready to quit when one of the fellas, Bongo, swam up to me. He said that he had seen some crayfish out further near the edge of the white water inshore of the rocks that separated the pool from the open ocean.

I swam out with him in a current that was so strong that it was laying the bull kelp flat along the bottom. I did not give a thought as to how I was going to get back against that current.

I came out of the current at the edge of the white water, and Bongo popped up with a tiny crayfish in his hand. But, as I attempted to dive, I found that my legs wouldn't move, and I suddenly felt very weak. I was physically exhausted.

I said to Bongo, "I am in trouble, mate, I can't move." He looked at me with a concerned look on his face and said, "Mate, I can't swim you back against this current; you're going to have to swim."

He was not letting me go; he was asking me to dig deep and pull myself together. I felt myself being pulled towards the open ocean and certain death by the current, so I had to do something very quickly.

The first thoughts were that I was not going to make it. I was going to be sucked through the rocks into the ocean, and I was going to drown. I knew that I couldn't be rescued by the others. I was fucked.

Bobbing around and drifting faster toward the channel to the ocean, I thought of my family – all the things you hear and read about that flash through someone's mind as they are about to die. My death was not going to be an accident. It was my stupidity that put me in this position.

I did not get to the stage of giving up, but I couldn't see how I could get back to shore. I looked all around me for some way out of this fix. I had never been in a situation like this before, but I had read things about it, so I started to think back on those things.

Bongo stayed with me, but he was getting concerned. 'C'mon, Dirty. You can do it," he said. My legs were dead in the water, though. I simply couldn't move them. I had to think.

I figured that if the current was taking me out, the waves could take me back. I noticed a semi-submerged rock about 20 yards inshore with a large piece of ribbon kelp attached to the top. As the waves broke over the rock, the kelp stretched several meters towards another rock further inshore. I noticed that after the wave passed, the current brought the kelp back towards the ocean. That piece of kelp was my lifeline. If I could reach it, I could grab hold and let the next wave carry me over the rock and sling me towards the next.

As the next breaking wave came towards me, I kicked with the last of my strength to get my legs to the surface so I could surf it towards the kelp. That wave carried me to the piece of kelp, which I grabbed in a stranglehold. I crashed into the rock and held on against the current to wait for the next wave.

I felt the surge of the current and hoped like hell that the kelp did not break. I saw the next rock I needed to get to. I watched and waited for the next big wave.

As the wave came, I let go of the kelp and surfed it to the next rock. I made it and noticed that the current was not quite as strong. All of a sudden, I thought I could make it, which I did, eventually.

When I made it to the beach, I could hardly walk. I had pulled muscles in my thighs, hamstrings, lower back, and shoulders. It took me weeks of massage therapy to heal.

I don't have nightmares, but as I went to sleep, I dreamt of being in the water and being sucked under by the weight of bull kelp. It made me sit bolt upright in bed so quickly, it disturbed Bongo in the bed next to me sufficient for him to ask me if I was alright.

Six months later, I was in deep water again, but in another country – New Zealand.

I was attending the 1994 Royal New Zealand Police College, Inspector's Qualifying Course, which was conducted over three months.

Considerable emphasis was placed on executive health and physical fitness, so I trained for months in preparation for the course. The last assessment on the course was called the 'Enduro,' which was like a triathlon on steroids.

In the first month, we were tested for our personality profiles, and a psychologist was assigned full time to the course at that time. Before we got into the course's academic component, we completed an outdoor management, leadership, and personal development course conducted between the 9th and 18th March 1994. The aim was to take each of us out of our normal safety net and observe our fear and stress responses.

We were told that we would participate in activities where some of us would be strong when others would be weak. But the situations would change, and we would see the reverse happen.

Apart from being one of the most exhilarating experiences of my life, it was an epiphany experience that has strongly influenced my life ever since.

I learned that a team is made up of people with different strengths and weaknesses. Good leadership is the ability to assign tasks accordingly. I learned that I could rely on others who I thought were weak to support me when my moments of weakness aligned with their moments of strength.

I learned that I could do things that I wouldn't have thought were possible; all it takes is the courage to work through my fear.

After five days into the course, we had hiked who knows how many miles through a volcano range and rough camped. There were constant problem-solving and leadership exercises used to punctuate every activity we undertook.

We were lectured by experts on personality and leadership. There were team-building exercises that would frighten the shit out of you, but we had to complete them because if we failed or refused, the team would lose points.

The course was mostly made up of the typical law enforcement personalities: they were logical, unemotional, and pragmatic types. Only a couple were the 'brains trust,' and they took the ribbing they got in good fun. They were the intellectual, feeling type personalities.

We had bonded as one big team, and I have no doubt that despite the personality and skill differences, there was a whole lot of mutual respect – for that part of the course, at least.

The day came for kayaking on the Waikato River below Lake Taupo. Before getting into the kayaks, we had to jump into the raging river above the Full James Rapids.

We traveled to the rapids on a bus. I heard one of the instructors on the bus mutter to another something about how full the river was, but it did not mean anything to me at the time. We had been at this boy scout stuff for a week, and we were pumped full of adrenalin, waiting for the next exciting challenge.

We arrived at a little beach below the rapids where the river was several hundred meters wide, or so it seemed to me.

Before getting in the kayaks, we were told that we had to ride the rapids without a boat. We were told to pair up a strong swimmer with a weak swimmer. As we walked to a canyon above the rapids, some of the fellows who knew about this adventure activity were muttering how dangerous it was and that "people drowned doing this shit."

We were fully clothed with only a kayak floatation vest for buoyancy.

A couple of local guides were hired for this exercise, and they told us how to get through the rapids without drowning. We were told that there was just one place we had to aim for. It was a big plume of water, but there was a submerged boulder underneath. We had to make sure our feet were above the water or risk being trapped on the boulder. Charming!!

We were told that the eddy might pull some of us back to the rapids, but we would eventually come out of it. The two guides would be on the river to help anyone who got into difficulty.

We stood at the edge of the cliff, looking down into the seething river. This was going to be sheer lunacy.

My swim buddy asked me which one of us jumped first. I looked at him and said, "You first. If you get into trouble, I am not going to be able to swim back against that current to get you."

I had a waterproof camera strapped to my wrist and was looking forward to the thrill. John jumped in and I followed him.

The first thing I noticed was how aerated the water was, and it took a bit of effort to get back to the surface. John was probably not more than 10 meters in front and traveling well with his feet above the water in front of him. I settled back and started taking photos before entering the plume that we had to aim for.

John disappeared as he was sucked down into the plume before being shot out the other side in no time.

I went into the plume with my feet in the air, and I felt my backside hit something solid. I thought it must have been someone else in there.

The trouble was that I did not come out on the other side. I was stuck with the full force of the water, pushing me onto the rock and forcing my head to my knees.

Before I had time to realize what was happening, another bloke plowed into my back, knocking me off the rock and out the other side. We bobbed up together, and he said, "Where'd you come from Dundee?" I said, "back in there somewhere," and we were laughing about it as we drifted out to the edge of the eddy.

We started breast stroking towards the beach, but as Ceps (his nickname given because of his skinny biceps) pulled away from me, I was pulled back into the eddy. I said, "see you on the beach; it feels like I am going for another ride."

Next thing, I went under the water for no apparent reason. I kicked back to the surface without being unduly concerned, but I was dragged straight back down again, only much deeper this time. It took almost all my strength to pull

CONTROL ALL FEAR

back to the surface, and I knew if I went under like that again, I probably did not have the strength needed to make it back to the surface.

The memory of my near-drowning experience on the west coast in Tasmania flashed through my mind. However, this was not as bad – yet.

As I broke the surface, I put my arm up and called for help from one of the guides on the other side of the eddy, about 20 meters away. I saw him look at me before I went down for the final time.

The surface water was crystal clear, but it became darker the deeper I was pulled down. The sound in my ears was a pinging sound, like sonar, and I could see little bubbles coming off my body rising to the surface. My life was flashing before my eyes, and I thought about going back to Australia in a steel casket. I thought about my family and the embarrassment I was about to cause the Tasmania Police.

Whatever depth I sank to, the water was dark green, virtually black, and the surface was out of sight. The bubbles in front of my face let me know that I was sinking straight downwards, not drifting down-stream.

This experience was much worse than Tasmania because I was under the water this time, not on top.

My breath was running out. I wondered how far it was to the bottom, and I wondered if drowning was going to be painful. I imagined that the first lung full of water was going to hurt like hell. I thought about how long it would take me to die after that?

Suddenly and deliberately, I turned my thoughts to survival.

Remembering what had happened to me in Granville Harbor, I did not fight the current; I couldn't afford to injure myself. I focused on the bubbles, so I knew which direction the surface was.

I thought my shoes were dragging me down, and I needed to get them off. As I brought my knees up towards my chest and started feeling for my boot laces, I noticed it was gradually becoming lighter. I realized I was floating upwards.

As the light grew brighter, I saw a red shape forming above. It was the guide's kayak, and I could see that he was looking down into the water. He was looking for me. My lungs felt like they were on fire, and I knew I was going to swallow water at any second. I felt angry. I was so fucking close to the surface. Couldn't I hang in for that last few meters?

My lungs felt like they were bursting, my ears were ringing, my brain felt like it was swelling in my skull, and my mind felt like it was going dim. The physical urge to take a breath was over-riding my mental capacity to keep my mouth shut.

80

I was close to the kayak with my arms reaching upwards towards it. I was so close, but my mouth opened involuntarily, and I took a large gulp of water. I tried to gag it in my throat, but some water made it into my lungs. If I could control my gag reflex, I could make it – I was so close. I squeezed the water out of my mouth with my cheeks.

I used my outstretched arms to gauge the distance to the kayak. I had one last chance before my mouth was going to open, so I kicked my legs with every ounce of energy I had left. I was so bloody close, but so bloody far away.

My mouth opened for what felt like the final time. I sucked water into my lungs, about two feet from the surface. In that instant, I thought I was going to sink to the bottom again, so I kicked harder. The physical effort hurt my chest immensely, but I suppose it was the water in my lungs.

Then I came up at the back of the kayak. I spewed out as much water as I could, and I grabbed the end of the kayak in the strongest bear-hug I could muster and wrapped my legs around it like I was a greyhound shagging a coke bottle. I was not going to let it go, no way and no how!

As I continued to spew out the water I had swallowed, the guide asked if I was OK. I don't think I answered him. I concentrated on spewing out every last drop of water I swallowed because of the risk from the giardia parasite that lives in the water in New Zealand. To me, getting rid of any parasites out of my lungs was my new priority. Getting me to shore was the guide's problem, and I wanted to get out of that fucking river fast.

The guide paddled me to shore past one of the older members who was floating on his back. He was totally exhausted, floating in an eddy close to shore. He looked fucked and was moaning, "I am gunna die, I am gunna die." It was Bruce, and he was the first bloke I met when I arrived, and we had become great friends.

The guide asked if I could swim the last 50 meters to shore so he could rescue Bruce. Indelibly etched in my mind's eye is the moment I looked at Bruce and thought, "Sorry, mate," and told the guide to take me to shore.

I truly thought I was letting Bruce die so I could save myself. However, I did not want to tackle the current again; I only let go of the kayak go about 15 yards from shore so the guide could recover Bruce.

The two guides were kept busy for probably half an hour, pulling blokes out of that whirlpool and bringing them close to shore.

Some had to be carried all the way, and some could swim once they were out of the whirlpool. Watching from the shore, I wondered if anyone was going to drown, especially the older members of the course. The thought of one of us drowning out there was upsetting as we watched helplessly from the beach. As they came close, we went out to help those who were distressed and struggling.

Everyone made it alive and physically unharmed, but not mentally unharmed.

I learned some years later that some of the men got PTSD as a result of the whirlpool experience. A few were pensioned out of the Police Force. I was told that one of them, an instructor, couldn't even walk past a swimming pool anymore.

These two experiences supported what I had been taught during special forces training. Don't give up until all your breath has gone, think through the problem, and stay positive – you can survive.

CONCLUSION

One thorn of experience is worth a wilderness of warning.

— William Shakespeare

There had to be a limit on how many stories I should use in this book, and this is it. I selected these stories because they were significant in taking me along the path to control my fear.

My addiction to the adrenaline rush and excitement developed as I learned that I could overcome the things I was afraid. There is excitement in facing danger, and there pleasure in achieving something good out of it.

Perhaps extreme sports where a mismanaged mistake or accident could result in death is a reasonable comparison to how I treated my job. The main difference between them is that my motivation was a combination of personal achievement as well as the desire to protect and serve someone else.

I wanted to be the best of the best. I did not want to confront a situation that I couldn't cope with. I wanted to be the calmest one among the chaos. I wanted to always have a plan at my fingertips. I did not want to be taken out or beaten up by any crook, ever! And, I did not want to ever be found guilty of breaking the law no matter how hard I enforced it.

I am hoping that I have told my stories in a way that shows how I grew from a naïve and frightened young man, way out of my depth, to a person confident in making wise choices when faced with adversity.

As a trainer and consultant for many years on matters relating to aggression and violence, I have found that fear is the first obstacle people need to overcome when they feel threatened.

Now I want to share what I learned about fear and what I did to overcome it.

Obviously, this is not all there is to know on the subject, nor is it all that I have read and used in my own development. If, on its own, it helps a reader, I will be very happy. If it encourages other readers to search for further and better information to help them, I will be just as happy. My purpose is achieved if this material helps someone face up to fear in someway or another.

PART TWO –
UNDERSTANDING
FEAR

INTRODUCTION

There are two kinds of fears: rational and irrational- or in simpler terms, fears that make sense and fears that don't.

— Daniel Handler

Fear is not a trivial matter. In many ways, it restricts our lives; it can imprison us. Fear can make us do things we know that we should not do or not do things that we know we should do.

Fear is used as a tool of oppression by people who are hungry for power over others. Those people know the power of fear, and they exploit it.

I became vastly more confident in everything I set out to do once I understood that fear is healthy when it is rational and controlled.

Becoming afraid in the face of real danger is normal; staying afraid is debilitating. To deny fear and to avoid dealing with it has harmful consequences that I discuss later.

Fear has two extremes. At one extreme, we freeze. We become immobilized, mentally and physically. At the other extreme, we panic. Our movements are frantic and irrational, and our mind goes into hyperdrive. How do we find the path through those extremes?

The starting point is to look back objectively over your own experience. Ask yourself, "What are these fears telling me? What am I trying to avoid? What is it that I am terrified of?" Remember back to a time when you were terrified. What sensations did you feel? What kind of thoughts raced through your mind? How did you respond? Did you panic? Did you freeze? Did you push on and hope for the best? Did you get angry? Did you make a calm, rational decision and overcome what it was you faced?

At this stage of the journey, you will be using your own experience to answer those questions.

Do you think your fears are rational or irrational? Most people could make a good argument that all their fears are rational. However, often our fears are irrational. When we know where they really come from, we can start to control them.

NATURAL FEAR

I am not afraid of death, but I am afraid of dying.

— Derek Jarman

Experts tell us that the anxious feeling we get when we are afraid is a natural biological reaction to a perceived threat. The symptoms or feelings we get are much the same, whether we are afraid of being bitten by a snake, getting into a fight, or getting our taxes audited.

Karl Albrecht Ph.D. says that there are five basic fears. He describes them in this way:

Extinction - the fear of annihilation, of ceasing to exist. In other words, the fear of death.

Mutilation - the fear of losing any part of our bodily structure, the thought of having our body's boundaries invaded, or of losing the integrity of any organ, body part, or natural function. Anxiety about animals, such as bugs, spiders, snakes, and other creepy things, arises from fear of mutilation.

Loss of Autonomy - the fear of being immobilized, paralyzed, restricted, enveloped, overwhelmed, entrapped, imprisoned, smothered, or otherwise controlled by circumstances beyond our control. It is commonly known as claustrophobia in physical form, but it also extends to our social interactions and relationships.

Separation - the fear of abandonment, rejection, separation; of becoming unwanted, disrespected, or not valued by anyone else.

Ego-death - the fear of humiliation, shame, self-disapproval, loss of integrity; the fear of losing one's constructed sense of attractiveness, capability, and worthiness.

Those are deliberately broad categorizations under which most of our fears can be listed.

Scott Mattison, a veteran of law enforcement in the USA, summarized the reasons for fear more directly by using words starting with the letter D.

- **Death:** Accidental, negligence, or murder.
- **Dying:** Lingering death from injury or illness.
- **Disability:** Physical, emotional, or
- **Dishonor/Disgrace;** doing the wrong thing. financial.
- **Dread:** Thinking the worst.
- **Discipline:** Punishment for an act or omission.
- **Despair:** Giving up without trying.
- **Denial:** Ignoring your vulnerability or weaknesses.
- **Defeat:** Setbacks and failure.

Most of us could relate to all of these with varying levels of fear. Recognizing that these are natural fears should lead us to accept that we experience them to some degree or another. The thing to think about is how to reduce the fear that causes anxiety or stress.

Fear might naturally subside with time or distance from whatever it is that stimulates it.

However, it can also subside when we actively explore the unknown aspect of the object, circumstances, or context that triggers the fear.

Gathering information and getting gentle, progressive exposure can enable us to adapt to situations that cause anxiety.

IRRATIONAL FEAR

Fear is harmful when it makes you irrational. Irrational fear makes you jump to conclusions about consequences that may never happen. Irrational fear holds you back.

— Author

These are some other common fears that most people have at some time or another:

- Fear of authority
- Fear of losing out
- Fear of not failure
- Fear of loss
- Fear of changes
- Fear of judgment
- Fear of humiliation
- Fear of growing old
- Fear of being alone
- Fear of being hurt

Have you experienced any of these fears? I suspect that you will be able to relate to at least one or more of them at some point in time. I know I do. I have felt them all, even for just a short time or on a small, subconscious level.

Accepting and confronting fear has been useful in revealing my weaknesses, vulnerable areas, stereotypes, and prejudices. It enabled me to acknowledge that those factors existed in my thinking. This awareness helped me confront them honestly and use that knowledge to direct my personal development and strengthen my character.

The purpose of fear is to make us act. It motivates action. Sometimes the action to take is avoidance, sometimes it is preparation and always to focus your concentration.

I accept that there are some things that I am not physically or mentally capable of coping with, so I avoid those. These are things like scuba diving (fear of deep water) or skydiving (fear of heights), among other risky things that hold no appeal to me. Therefore, I learned that it is not necessary or wise to discard all fear completely.

Another reason that fear is useful is that it helps you to anticipate, prepare for, or react appropriately to a dangerous situation.

The challenge is not to allow fear to stop you from taking action or avoid dealing with something you should. Nor to allow fear to control you and provoke you to overreact and make rash decisions.

The training I received in the Special Operations Group was also eye-opening. I was surprised by how easy it is to control or influence your circumstances when you take control of fear. A sense of control is like an antidote for panic.

Thudong monks of South East Asia had a system to train novice monks to overcome fear and face reality with clear thinking. They were told that they will never know how much or how little they feared something until the monk actually faced his fears.

In the forests where they lived, the monks had to be cautious of constant danger and always be alert. One of the dangers they faced daily was from the tigers that lived in the forests where the monks walked.

The monks were first put with a teacher who took them through daily rituals, received instruction, and learned by observing. Next, they were sent into the forests, where they would spend the day walking and meditating. At night they slept alone on an elevated platform where they would cleanse their mind through meditation.

The theory was that a strong concentration on reality would develop or deepen at a critical moment and further wisdom or insight would occur.

The Thai monk, Ajahn Man, said about the battle between fear and reality, "If the fear is defeated, the mind will be overwhelmed by courage and enjoy profound inner peace."

Fear can give us great strength and unleash the tremendous response power of our basic survival instinct. Fear is, therefore, nothing to be afraid of.

Decide what you should be afraid of (awareness) and decide what you can do to take control of it.

MANIPULATED THROUGH FEAR

Fear is the best weapon of all great manipulators. It can move people to do anything, no matter how nonsensical it is. "Neither a man nor a crowd nor a nation can be trusted to act humanely or to think sanely under the influence of a great fear."

— Bertrand Russell

The story goes that Stalin plucked a live chicken in front of his commanders to demonstrate how easy it was to control dumb people. It caused the chicken great agony as its feathers were removed one by one. The floor became filled with blood and feathers in a puddled mass, with the frantic shrieks of the chicken filling the room in a fevered pitch.

After plucking the chicken of its feathers, Stalin began dropping bits of wheat after his footsteps as he walked around the room. The bird started following, gobbling up the bits of food. "See!" Stalin remarked, "Even though I have done the most terrible acts on this creature, it still follows me if it is given a small meaningless treat every now and then. This is how to govern stupid people."

Fear is the weapon of all great manipulators. It can move people to do anything, no matter how irrational it is.

While fear is useful in situations where the threat of immediate harm exists, it can cause paralysis of clear thinking, leading to irrational action. That, in turn, leads people to control a situation to the people they think have the power to solve their problem.

Around the world today, the artificial construction and maintenance of fear is used to make us believe that only they have the means and ability to protect us from a threat.

Generating fear is a tactic being used continuously in our everyday life. Still, most people appear to be unaware of it.

Politicians are elected by persuading the masses using fear. Companies are selling their products by manipulating consumers' insecurities through advertising. Journalists influence public opinion by terrorizing people's minds. There are many more examples of how societies are manipulated by fear if you chose to think about it.

Social media has given anyone the ability to propagate their negative narratives and engage in fearmongering to an extent never before seen in history.

Let's face it, people in positions of power, past and present, have effectively controlled certain aspects of society by encouraging people to be afraid. Mainstream and social media continually provoke fear in society by dramatizing situations to make people feel threatened.

Causing public hysteria over a perceived problem often results in the passing of legislation that is highly punitive, unnecessary, and serves to justify the agendas of those in positions of power, authority, and influence.

Unnecessary fear is a tool to manipulate us and stop us from acting and reasoning rationally. When we cannot control our emotional response to what we read or hear, we become susceptible to manipulation.

Ignorance is the root of misfortune. Suppose we continue to be deceived by those who manipulate our fears for their benefit. In that case, we will suffer the consequences of ill-health, negativity, and loss of faith, loss of freedom, and loss of hope for the future.

If for no other reason, being able to control our emotional responses to the plethora of negativity and propaganda thrown at us every day is a great reason to learn how to control fear.

Truthfully, my opinion about people who I know that get sucked into this is no one's business, but it isn't flattering.

DON'T PANIC

Fear and panic are two separate emotions. Fear's healthy, panic is deadly.

— Gerard Butler as 'Frosty.'

Fear is not panic. Panic is the condition of being overwhelmed by fear. The typical response to panic is one of the three basic self-defense instincts - flight, fight, freeze (Barlow, 1988).

Panic is the sudden onset of intense fear that reaches a peak within minutes and includes one or more of the following symptoms: tremors, pounding heart, or highly accelerated heart rate; sudden sweating; shaking limbs, and shortness of breath or feeling unable to breathe.

The types of responses you might see from a person in panic are extremes of the primary defense instincts:

Flight: Blindly run away, possibly tripping over or bumping into things, no clear direction, the aim is to get away as far and fast as possible.

Fight: Intense or hysterical rage, screaming, punching, scratching, biting, kicking. Irrational physical motion to attack the perceived threat.

Freeze: Immobility, unable to move, staring vacantly ahead, curled in a ball on the ground, hide their eyes from the threat, whimpering or sobbing, inability to function physically or mentally.

Panic is an unreasoning, unjustified terror which paralyzes you from making the efforts to change our attitude from giving up to survival.

You can control panic if you recognize the warning signs and symptoms mentioned above.

The first step is educating yourself. Learning about how fear works on the brain can empower you to recognize a panic attack for what it is: an over-stimulation of the amygdala, causing a surge of adrenaline. The stimulation is normal, but you do not want too much of it.

Building knowledge about fear and its effect on the brain and body is probably the least understood, but most important, step towards controlling fear.

On the other hand, most people will be aware of the other steps that need to be taken to control panic.

Calm breathing: Controlling your breathing helps prevent hyperventilation and building up carbon dioxide in your blood. Taking a couple of deep breaths and then making sure you continue to breathe normally during exposure to danger helps you to think clearly and react appropriately.

I often found myself starting to involuntarily breathe shallowly and feel my muscles tensing before entering a danger zone. I remember my first martial arts tournament. The coach's advice before going into the ring was to make sure I kept breathing. It seemed like strange advice at the time, but I quickly understood what he meant as soon as the fight started. I could hear him shouting from the corner, "breath, breath!"

He could see that I had become tense, and as soon as I started breathing, my muscles relaxed, and I was able to win the fight.

Apart from that example, there were many times that I was told to take a deep breath, and I found it to work every time. From simple things like entering a court to give evidence, attending a brawl, or preparing to enter a stronghold to arrest an armed offender. Deep, controlled breathing worked every time to calm my mind and relax my body to get ready for action.

Relax the muscles: Muscles in the neck and shoulder tend to tense up first in my experience. Sometimes I can feel my toes curl up, and my fists clench involuntarily to the point of being painful.

Combined with controlled breathing, deliberately tensing and relaxing the muscles lowers tension and stress. Sometimes this is literally 'mind over matter,' so you have to focus your mind on breathing and relaxing the muscles. I have read that you start at the feet and gradually work your way up the body, muscle by muscle. However, I have found it useful to focus on where I feel the most tension, especially the muscles that I will need to respond to the situation.

Unclutter your thinking: You might find that your mind is racing and all sorts of thoughts are going through your brain. You must get rid of negative thoughts and focus on solutions to the problem. These need to be positive thoughts, thoughts of success, or victory. Nothing else matters except your survival.

In the stories I have told, I attempted to give a good description of the thoughts that have raced through my mind, good and bad. I learned to dismiss negative 'what if' thoughts quickly. As new adversity comes my way, I am conscious of getting rid of negative thoughts as fast as possible. Sometimes it is not easy, but it must be done.

Meditation is one way of getting rid of negative thoughts. The more time you have before a crisis strikes, the more time you have to meditate on positive thoughts. For spiritual people, use this time to pray and recognize faith and hope as your focus point.

Be prepared: Know the types of danger that you could face and prepare yourself physically and mentally to respond to it. Physical training in particular skills is essential, along with maintaining a reasonable level of physical fitness. Mentally rehearsing what you would do if a situation eventuates is also crucial.

Being prepared to deal with risk or danger gives you confidence and faith in your own ability to survive. You will still be afraid, but you will not panic.

Being prepared for anything is not difficult if you follow a systematic process to acknowledge your fear, acquire knowledge, and develop suitable physical and mental skills.

COURAGE AND COWARDICE

"But the bravest are surely those who have the clearest vision of what is before them, glory and danger alike, and yet notwithstanding, go out to meet it."

— Thucydides The Peloponnesian War

I don't like the word hero when describing people doing the job they are trained to do. Heroism should be reserved for people who master fear and cope with *extraordinary* danger.

The dictionary defines "hero" as "a person of distinguished courage or ability, admired for his or her brave deeds and noble qualities." To me, heroes are more than a courageous person; they show great bravery over and over again.

A courageous person acts despite fear.

Courage is usually found in the person who believes in themselves and what they stand for. They are better prepared to cope with fear because they understand the situation. They use all their knowledge and skill and show incredible mental strength to do everything they must to overcome a challenge. They are confident in their ability to meet the challenges they face. They are passionate and have a purpose.

Anyone can find courage when circumstances demand it, but people can do stupid things and be thought to be courageous. Like being a non-swimmer jumping into a swollen river to save someone – that is sheer stupidity, not courage.

That leads me to bravery. To be brave means taking all your knowledge, training, and experience and applying it to the situation you are confronted with and choosing the right course of action. Bravery is courage, plus wisdom.

Courageous people have these traits in common.

They have conviction. You will always know where a courageous person stands and what they stand for. They have beliefs and values that they are passionate about. Their actions are consistent, and their behavior is predictable when trouble comes their way.

Self-confident. People who believe in themselves know who they are and what they stand for.

Integrity. They know the difference between right and wrong. These are honorable people who live out their values publicly and privately every day. They talk the talk and walk the walk.

Empathetic and compassionate. They are understanding of other people's needs and put them above their own when necessary.

Objective. Fair-minded, even-handed, and open-minded. They approach challenges openly and honestly and have no difficulty in justifying the decision they make.

Strength in adversity. A courageous person accepts a challenge. They are not afraid to challenge the status quo and take calculated risks to find a solution to a challenge. They are persistent and won't quit.

Embrace the unknown. They use wisdom to make decisions when they don't fully understand what lies ahead and act accordingly. They use their instincts if they lack all the information, they would like to make a good decision.

Leadership. Not overly concerned with what people think of them, the courageous person leads the way into adversity, motivating and supporting others to find their courage to follow.

Action. You see more action than you hear words from the courageous person. Their actions and the results they achieve speak louder than their words.

Cowardice is the opposite of courage. It is found in people who let fear and excessive self-concern override doing or saying what is right, good, and helpful to others or themselves in the face of danger.

Imagine for a moment that you have trained hard with an individual to do a risky job. You have shared stories, developed skills, talked the talk, and can't wait to put it all to the test. The day comes to get the job done, and you find that the other person goes to water and refuses to back you up. You either go it alone or you come up with another plan to accommodate the coward.

Cowardice is not being overwhelmed by fear. Cowardice is the conscious choice of turning your back on a situation, leaving someone else at risk. It is a deliberate unwillingness to take a calculated risk.

Cowardice is an insidious form of dishonesty. A coward hides their fear, lack of confidence, and over-riding desire for self-preservation behind a cover of toughness and bravery – they talk the talk but will not walk the walk.

Cowardice is revealed in the heat of a moment. A coward is a person who refuses to do something that they can do because they are more concerned about self-preservation rather than doing what is right.

A person who freezes when they are suddenly attacked or confronted with a crisis they have not prepared for, is not a coward. Nor is the person who is forced into a role or situation for which they are not suited.

People who are overwhelmed in a crisis can be understood, but not if they are a person who has boasted about how good they are.

I contemplated writing about my experience with cowards I have met, but I decided against it. On the one hand, I feel sorry for the people they have conned with their tough talk. On the other hand, I am grateful that the people they have fooled have not had the same, or worse, experiences with them. Instead, I will describe the common traits I have seen in the cowards I have met and worked with.

The first trait in those people I have met is an irrational fear. They were unable to think logically through a challenge, and they tried to cover up their fear. Those people put a stern expression on their faces, spoke in short, sharp sentences, and talked tough.

They acted as though they were all-knowing and in charge of something important and that looking stern was the way to stay in charge of it. This type of person talks a good fight on the training ground or in the office when there is no danger.

Looking into these people's eyes, you can see something missing. Their gaze is not steely nor focused when their eyes should be alert and filled with confidence and concentration. Instead, there is a vacuum behind their gaze. They use their stern tone of voice to discourage questions being asked of them, the answers to which they don't have.

Other cowardly traits that I have seen include:

They fear being exposed for what they are. They know their true character isn't worth a damn to others, so they lie and creates a false image. They act to elevate themselves on an illusionary pedestal to tower over others.

They avoid competing head to head with stronger people. They have an inferiority complex towards good, strong, honest people. They are afraid of being called out on their bullshit. They can't hide and fight back that way. Instead, they are likely to make up lies to put the stronger person down in the eyes of their cohort. Secretly they admire and look up to strong people, but they can never make the same grade, or if they do, they fail when the chips are down.

They surround themselves with weak-minded people. Their cohort believes in the image the coward portrays, so he is a hero among them. Their cohort will be mostly people who are much less experienced or younger than them and who have never seen the coward in any real action.

They talk the big talk. In other words, they use strong words spoken with a stern look on their faces. They bank on cheap talk, and they use empty words to get their way and inflate their image among their peers. Cowards can possess excellent training skills and will show them off to make others believe that they will be hot shit when the balloon goes up. A brave person just takes action, makes things happen, and gets the job done. Their achievements on the front line speak for themselves.

They won't admit their weaknesses or apologize. Cowards fear their weaknesses being exposed, and they fear ridicule and disparaging remarks being made about them. They have endless excuses for when they screw up and will never apologize when they do.

They lay blames on everyone and everything else rather than accepting responsibility themselves. They can't face the truth that they are not as competent as they make out – it is always someone or something else's fault.

They are a crybaby and create excuses to hide the fact that they screwed up badly. They rely on their tears and excuses to stop others from seeing that they lack courage. They look for sympathy and soak it up like a sponge soaks up water.

They put on a show that has no end. I had a colleague who I thought was a friend. He is a great showman who I thought no one else could see through. However, I have met people who have worked with him since I had. It was refreshing to hear their stories of the cowardice and bullshit they had seen in him for themselves. All talk, no action, and full of bullshit is the common trait of a coward.

Cowards are bullies. In the workplace, they use whatever position, power, or influence they have, to prevent or disrupt others from advancement or achievement.

I have observed them use their position to downgrade competent people on training and selection courses who were potentially better than them. I can speak from experience in this too. Once I was told by my Commander that the reason I was being screwed by two senior officers was that they considered me a threat to them. It made sense at the time too.

So many great officers I worked with were screwed in the same way by the police hierarchy and unjustly had their careers ruined because they did not pander to the bullies.

Cowards won't take on a challenge alone. This is where a lot of the traits come together. Taking responsibility on their own shoulders is an anathema to the coward. They need to surround themselves with people that they can blame for their failures and screw-ups.

The coward lacks confidence in their ability, and self-preservation is their main focus. They can swim and want to jump in the pool, but they don't want to get wet.

They are passive-aggressive people. Anything goes that can be done to elevate their self-esteem and lower others. The coward uses sarcasm, insults, threats, rumor, gossip, and obstructive behavior to make them look superior.

Online, the coward cuts loose behind false identities. In the workplace, they lurk around in the background, and face to face, they are sly and conniving. They are also likely to sulk and lament if they don't get their own way.

They fight back to cover up their cowardice, not because they are right. They use passive-aggressive behavior to divert attention from their own behavior. They will take delight in pointing out your previous mistakes, or failures, to validate their argument. They will do and say almost anything to defend themselves; whether it is truth or fiction doesn't matter to them.

So, let me finish this chapter by repeating that courage is not the absence of fear; it is what you do despite it.

Thucydides hits the nail on the head, talking about the bravest are surely those who have the clearest vision of what is before them. This is the absolute core of what this book is about – know what is ahead of you, anticipate and assess the risks, the danger, the worst possible outcome, and train yourself to act and survive.

We don't need another hero; what we need is courageous people.

FEAR AND SYMPTOMS

You gain strength and confidence by every experience in which you really stop and look fear in the face. You must do the thing that you think you cannot do.

— Eleanor Roosevelt

Many people ignore their fear. I have seen people in a state of sheer terror who have denied that they were afraid. They had every right to be scared but the problem was that they were ashamed to admit it. Some I have seen have wanted to show how tough they were. Sadly, on too many of those occasions, I saw those people fold under pressure. Some showed cowardice, and others were unable to function properly. I saw one person literally shit their pants, and others break down and cry uncontrollably.

There have been times that I did not admit that I was scared too. Especially when I was leading people into danger. But I realized how stupid that was when I learned that you cannot hide the physical symptoms of fear. If I wanted my colleagues to have confidence in me, I needed to control my fear and convert it into confidence. So, let us look briefly at the symptoms of fear. See how many you can recognize in yourself.

Fear is created when our sense of vulnerability is triggered by an unusual or threatening circumstance that we feel we have little or no control over.

Fear, once triggered, spreads far and wide in the human body. Up top, in our brains, the amygdala is responsible for registering frightful stimuli and triggering a response in the nervous system.

According to literature, the hypothalamus flushes the bloodstream with the stress hormones cortisol and adrenaline. This causes your heart rate to increase and lungs to dilate, allowing more oxygen into the system.

Organs that prove unnecessary in a life-or-death situation, like the gastrointestinal system, shrink. This can cause people to lose control of their bladder or bowel or vomit. Every other resource is sent to the muscles, which you'll need for a flight or fight response.

The chain reaction that starts in the brain with a stressful stimulus and ends with the release of chemicals can cause your heart to beat rapidly. Your breathing will become fast and shallow, and your muscles can become tense.

One or more of five emotional reactions are triggered. These include confusion, aversion, a sense of weakness, the feeling of danger, and a need to run away.

These reactions prepare us for choosing the best defense response; flight, fight, or freeze.

The stimulus can be anything that we believe can hurt us. It could be a spider, a knife at your throat, an auditorium full of people waiting for you to speak, or the sound of a car backfiring, among a plethora of other things.

Fear can be a weakness if it is not brought under control, especially if it leads to panic. It impacts our ability to think clearly and make wise decisions about how to cope with a situation. On occasions, it can make us act instinctively without thinking. For example, a person might jump or duck their head when they hear a sudden loud noise before asking themselves, "what was that, and should I react to it?"

You might leap in the air when you think you are about to step on a snake, only to find it was a piece of rubber hose that frightened you.

It is not uncommon to experience auditory and visual distortions in critical incidents that cause great fear.

Sounds may diminish, and we may not hear loud noises, such as gunshots that would typically disrupt our concentration. For others, sounds are louder, enabling a finer tuning into a danger. Visual distortions can occur that can help us. We can experience tunnel vision: an intense, focused concentration, usually on what is perceived to be the danger, with little or no attention paid to peripheral vision. Also, we might see more visual details with greater clarity than usual.

As I mentioned in my stories, I have experienced these distortions myself.

Another distortion I experienced was in the bush during a night operation at a siege. The night was so dark that our night vision goggles were not operating at their best. That was because there was no ambient light. There was mist in the air to make visibility even worse.

This environment meant that my visual senses were overtaken by my hearing. I couldn't depend on seeing the suspect in the bush until he was on top of us, so I depended on hearing him approach us. My hearing was so focused that I could hear the mist on the leaves in the trees.

On another occasion, many years ago, I was taking a bank teller statement who was the victim of a bank robbery. The witness gave a detailed description of the weapon used and described the barrel as though it were a 12-gauge shotgun. However, she could not describe the mask the robber wore. Another teller gave a great description of the robber's physical features but little about the weapon.

The witness who described the large barrel on the weapon was more afraid of being shot than the other witness who was more concerned about describing the robber. Therefore, her vision was distorted by the threat she perceived from the end weapon.

On another occasion, I was investigating an armed robbery of a pedestrian in the city center. The robbery occurred around 0830 hours on a weekday when people were walking to work.

The victim said the robber attacked her from behind and put a knife to her throat and demanded money. She said the knife was a kitchen knife. It had a serrated blade and bone handle. The clothing worn by the robber was purple trousers, a yellow shirt, and a plaid sports coat. He was aged in his late 50s.

This was a weird description, but the victim, a young woman, was sure it was accurate. Having learned my lesson about trusting people's perceptions years earlier, I broadcast the description over the patrol car radio. Naturally, I received some smart-arse comments about looking for someone that lived in the 1970s or a hippy of some sort. One person commented that Beau Brummel must have reincarnated and come to town.

Within the hour, the offender was in custody. He had absconded from the mental health facility, which, at that time, was located in a town 40 kilometers away.

These perceptual distortions are normal and common for people to experience during a critical incident, and they can be helpful.

However, perceptual distortions have other characteristics that are important to be aware of. Due to tunnel vision, a person may not perceive details, such as other peripheral actions on the periphery. Later, a person may be able to recall or describe only those aspects of the situation that they were focused upon and, therefore, be unreliable witnesses for other factors of the situation.

A person may not be able to give an accurate description of the time that transpired due to time distortion. Because of auditory distortion, some people may not hear certain details, such as how many shots were fired.

Realize that perceptual distortions are normal and occur automatically and unconsciously under peak stress conditions. Therefore, people's accounts of what they saw, heard, felt, smelt, or touched will most likely be different from another's.

Why is it important to understand these distortions? Suppose you are a police officer interviewing witnesses. In that case, you must realize that no two people will be able to make the same statement of evidence about an event.

On a personal level, you need to acknowledge that other people may not have had the same experience as you did. This is most important if you are talking to someone who suffers critical incident or post-trauma stress. It is a grave mistake to dismiss a person's perception of a traumatic event based on your own ideas of what you perceived or what you might or might not think happened.

Never ever judge a person on their personal experience of a traumatic incident based on your perceptions of an incident.

FIGHT, FLIGHT, FREEZE RESPONSE

There is a time to fight, a time to flee, and a time to do nothing. At any moment in time, only one of those is the safest option. Choose wisely.

— Author

We have all heard about the fight or flight response to danger, but not so many know about the third response: freeze.

The fight-flight-freeze response is your body's natural reaction to danger. It's a type of stress response that helps you react to perceived threats, like an oncoming car or growling dog.

Have you ever noticed how you feel after a sudden frightening experience has passed? For example, after a near-miss while driving, or after being startled by a dog that barks savagely at you?

These are situations that most of us have experienced. We react so fast that we don't really have to think about what we need to do. We swerve and hit the brakes in a vehicle to avoid a collision, but then we need to pull over to catch our breath.

As you walk peacefully past a house, you hear a dog suddenly rush towards you, barking viciously. Before you even look, you have jumped to one side to distance yourself from the sound. Then you realize you are safe because the dog is behind a gate, but you need to stop to catch your breath.

Did you notice the funny feeling inside your body, sort of like a cold sensation? Did you notice that your breathing becomes deeper, and your hands and knees shake?

The sudden fright causes adrenaline and other drugs to flood your system to make you hyper-focused on the perceived danger. This causes your nervous system to focus only on one thing, and everything else is held at bay.

The release of neurochemicals and hormones increases heart rate, breathing shunts blood away from the intestines, and sends more to the muscles for running or fighting.

Some people react badly to danger and neither fight nor flee. They freeze up or run up and down on the same spot, screaming and waving their arms about. Others might simply collapse on the ground and huddle in a fetal position, whimpering helplessly.

In extreme cases, people can be 'scared to death.' The surge of adrenalin is too much for their heart to cope with.

The freezing response is more difficult for people to understand compared to fight or flight. Like fight or flight, freezing as a response can be explained by comparing it to animal instinct. For example, an animal being preyed on by a predator. When a prey animal is stalked by a predator, it might freeze in the expectation of the predator not seeing it. When it has been caught and overcome by a predator, it often eventually "freezes up" and becomes entirely still.

In humans, a state of 'freezing' makes our heart rate and breathing slow down, and we may find that we hold our breath. We may feel cold or numb, and we might experience a sense of being trapped within our bodies. Painkilling hormones can also be released into our system to reduce the event's physical and emotional impact.

Our memory may also be affected, leaving us struggling to remember part of or all of the experience.

After being scared, a person will sometimes be described as looking as "pale as a ghost." This is a normal reaction. There are other physical reactions that we might experience after a fright too.

I recall looking for my golf ball in a marshy area after a wayward shot. As I parted the grass, I uncovered a snake curled up. I reacted very slowly, allowing the grass to fall back over the snake, and I slowly stepped back onto the fairway, not taking my eyes off where the snake lay.

Once I realized the snake hadn't moved, I noticed that I needed to breathe – I had unconsciously held my breath all that time. I was so tense across my shoulders that it was painful. As I started to walk away, I felt pain in my feet. I had to stop and remember looking at my feet, wondering what was wrong. My toes had tightly curled up under my feet, and I needed to sit and relax my feet to untangle them.

Freezing can occur when the physical impact of our stress hormones is so great that they cause intense negative emotions like extreme shock, anxiety, panic, and terror. Feeling powerless to defend ourselves, the experience becomes too much for us to cope with, and our brain shuts down, enabling us to dissociate from the experience.

However, freezing (doing nothing or submitting) is an appropriate response in some cases. It is a response that can save your life and help you survive. For example, do not jump into a flooded river to save a drowning child if you cannot swim.

There are times when you have escaped danger but are tempted to go back into it to try and save someone else. All well and good if it is a calculated decision, but pure folly if it costs your life. My great mentor counseled me this way. He said, 'When Daniel got out of the lions' den, he did not go back for his hat."

I investigated a murder where a young woman's boyfriend was stabbed to death. The woman was dragged across the dead body, kidnapped, and taken into the forest to be killed after being raped by the murderer.

The young lady's courage continues to impress me. She submitted to the rape and negotiated with the offender to concoct a story about someone else committing the murder, so he would let her live. There is no doubt in my mind that her submission to him saved her life.

I could give many more examples from my personal experience where doing nothing or submitting was the best and the only course of action to take at the time.

People often ask me how you know whether to choose a flight or fight response, and others ask me how freezing in a dangerous situation help? The answer to those questions depends entirely on the individual. There is no specific answer because the right response depends on several coexisting factors in each individual case.

The best way I can answer those questions is to say, "stay calm, understand the situation, face the threat, and direct your energy on survival.

The system I have developed to cope with fear came about through my attempt to answer these questions for myself. The system has worked exceptionally well for me so far and encompasses that philosophy. But before we get to the system, we need to understand a little more about fear.

PART THREE –
STEPS TO TAKE
TO CONTROL
FEAR

CRITICAL INCIDENT SURVIVAL PROCESS

My mission in life is not merely to survive but to be at peace with myself, knowing that I reacted fast, efficiently, and effectively to cope with any adversity.

Some people have ways of thinking that motivate their will to survive. These people understand that emergencies and disasters can happen at any time. They ready themselves mentally and physically for tactical thought and action. This type of person has strong feelings about self-preservation.

Most people chose not to think about the bad things that can happen. Those people believe "it will never happen to me." They ignore danger and risks, hoping that it will never happen. The consequences for this type of thinking include death or injury, survival by good luck, and post-trauma stress.

Anticipation and preparation are the first steps to take to avoid becoming overwhelmed in a crisis.

The following diagram is an adaptation of Dr. Roger Solomon's dynamics of fear model that shows the psychological processes that people go through when they become involved in a critical incident.

BASED ON THE DYNAMICS OF FEAR MODEL
Courtesy of Dr Roger M Solomon Ph.D.

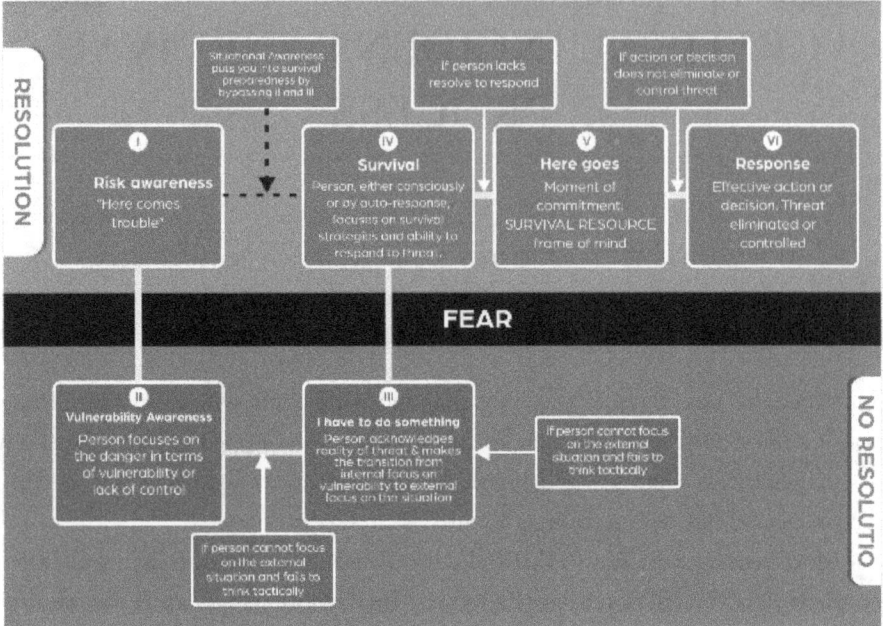

The process starts when a person first becomes aware of potential danger and ends with a response.

I have included blocking points between each phase. These are the places where people fail to progress – they freeze or fold under pressure.

Going through the full process when faced with imminent danger creates a dangerous time delay between recognizing the threat and taking action. The delay can be fatal.

Therefore, the concept of controlling fear in the face of immediate danger is to speed up your reaction time by going through phases II and III in advance of a crisis.

Here is how Dr. Roger Solomon describes the six phases.

Phase I. "Here comes trouble."
This phase starts the moment a person realizes the potential for a threat. You become alert, the body reacts as the natural "alarm reaction" starts the adrenaline

flow, and you focus your attention on the danger. Sometimes you can be thrust into a situation with no warning, and the process begins with the next phase.

The next phase begins as a person focuses on the threat and perceives that the danger is potentially life-threatening. This phase is adequately described as "Oh, shit!!"

Phase II. Vulnerability Awareness
This is the point that a person realizes that they are in deep trouble and have little or no control over what is happening.

People may experience a sense of shock and arousal, startle and surprise, disbelief and dread, and feelings of weakness and helplessness. You might have thoughts like these.

"Oh, my God. This can't be happening."
"This is not supposed to happen."
"I am going to die."
"What am I going to do?"
"I don't know what to do."
"I am not in control here."

Dr. Solomon says that when a person's focus is solely on danger and how vulnerable they are, they tend to feel weak and helpless (Bandura. 1986). The person feels he or she has little control over the situation.

This is a critical phase that needs to be overcome rapidly if you are to survive. Otherwise, fear, or vulnerability awareness, might win over rational thinking and control a person's responses at this point. Or fear at this point might instinctively drive survival responses into action. This is where decisions might be good or bad.

For some people, vulnerability awareness immediately leads to focusing on what they must do to survive or gain control of the situation. This is where some people jump directly to the fourth phase. These people have prepared themselves; and they know what needs to be done. They focus on the danger and what they can do to respond to it. These are the people that leave others standing in their wake with their jaws hanging slack as they get into action.

But sometimes you can be surprised by the unexpected, something you have never anticipated. The perception of vulnerability and lack of control can be overwhelming in extreme cases. If you are taken by surprise, and you stay focused on your weakness beyond the initial shock, your fear will increase uncontrollably. Distracting thoughts can occur and cloud your judgment.

Distracting thoughts disrupt your ability to respond to danger (Barlow, 1988). Likewise, if your attention remains focused on your physical reactions (shaking, blood pressure, etc.), the more you will be influenced by overwhelming emotions. Panic and mindless fight, flight, or freezing can result.

To move beyond this emotional bottleneck, you must go through a transition phase to focus on your response to the situation and survival.

You need to understand the situation and acknowledge the reality of what is happening. You have to drag your focus away from the fear of being hurt and the negative thoughts it brings.

At this point, you will realize that you have to do something if you are going to survive and meet the challenge of the situation.

Phase III.   "I've got to do something!"
Now you have acknowledged the reality of the threat. The shock, disbelief, and denial of what is happening have passed. I have found this phase to be exhilarating, regardless of how bad a situation was.

The ability to control fear enables people to refocus on a solution; their attention shifts from negative and defeatist thoughts to assessing what is happening around them. They stop denying the threat and being overwhelmed by it and start working on a solution.

They focus on reality instead of thinking about feeling helpless and afraid. You can see a person's facial expression change as they enter this phase. Tension is replaced by a steely resolve. They exude a calmness that many people misunderstand as carelessness. This person is acknowledging the reality of the threat and is no longer in shock or surprised. They are ready to act to solve the problem.

This transition enables them to focus on responding instead of feeling helpless and remaining frozen in place.

Speaking from my own experience, I get a feeling of detachment. I take little or no notice of everything unnecessary for my response to the situation. I ignore bullshit advice and pointless conversation, which often abounds, especially from panicked people.

Nothing before or after matters to me except what is right there in front of me. I become intensely focused and determined.

I have learned that this detachment is a psychological defense mechanism that suppresses feelings of shock and vulnerability. It causes those potentially overwhelming feelings to the back of my mind. Suppressing those feelings enables me to focus on functioning to get through the crisis.

This disassociation of emotions is characteristic of some people but not of others. People who react in this way need to know that it is normal in extreme stress situations, and they are not crazy.

I have read that this is an automatic response that cannot be taught. I disagree that it cannot be taught. I had to teach and train myself to disassociate from emotion to function through a crisis. Indeed, the purpose of this book is to help others do the same.

The faster you realize that you have to do something to meet a challenge, the quicker you enter the next phase: survival.

Phase IV.   Survival
At this point, you begin thinking about what has to be done to gain control of the situation - what can you do to survive. The better you are prepared for this type of decision making, the easier and faster it becomes.

Soldiers and police officers commonly describe how their training automatically comes to mind. Some think through several courses of action, and others just find themselves responding instinctively. This type of automatic response is typical of those who have trained and used mental rehearsal techniques (or drills) to prepare themselves for life-threatening situations.

In the early chapters, the stories I have told demonstrate how the thinking process can be remarkably rapid, as though they flood through your brain. I have described how my thinking sped up during moments of peak stress. Be aware, though, the actions and options you think about in less than a second can take minutes to articulate verbally and take pages to write in words.

Usually, at this moment, feelings of dread and helplessness change. As you see and think about the danger and your capability to respond to it, you feel more balanced and in control of the outcome.

Dr. Solomon describes another principle of human functioning that is occurring at this point. When a person views the danger or threat in terms of their capability to respond to it, feelings of dread and helplessness decrease, enabling them to cope and respond (Bandura. 1986; Lazarus and Folkman, 1984). The person feels more in control and can better maintain an external focus on dealing with the situation.

I cannot stress enough how important it is to take notice of this. It is a sense of confidence, control, and achievement that has helped me avoid critical-incident and post-trauma stress.

People prepared for coping with a crisis typically have a keen focus on what is happening externally. They will often experience tunnel vision, focusing solely on what they perceive to be the biggest threat.

All in the flash of a second or less, you will focus intensely on changes in the threat, prioritizing options, confirming what is happening, and anticipating events and their consequences.

The external focus is vital to survival because an inward focus on your sense of vulnerability can escalate fear and interfere with your ability to think clearly and respond.

The next phase is the "moment of resolve." That resolve comes once you commit to a course of action and start to do it. This is the "Here goes!" moment.

Phase V. "Here goes!"

This phase starts with your response to the crisis. Your response could be reasoned or instinctive. It is a powerful moment – the moment between realizing what you have to do and committing to it and starting to do it. Don't be concerned about an instinctive response. The more you are prepared, and the better you are trained, you can trust your automatic responses.

This is the moment of victory and survival, and you will have a strong, powerful mindset.

You might experience a level of strength that is not normal. You will feel great control over your strength. Although adrenaline is flowing and your body is mobilized and aroused, you will be in control. You will be committed to action and start to initiate it. Though thoughts will be racing, they tend to be clear and lucid. There is often a sense of heightened awareness and a feeling that you are not over or under-reacting. It will feel right.

Your sense of confidence will be strong at this moment. This is the survival resource frame of mind (Solomon, 1988). In other words, focusing on the capability to respond, rather than on feelings of vulnerability, leads to power. The resolve to respond when experiencing fear leads to tremendous strength. This is the way that fear can be used to make you much stronger than usual.

However, in other cases, a person may experience no conscious awareness of their survival strength.

I was only aware of my fear and how vulnerable I felt when responding in my early experience. Years later, after learning about fear and reflecting deeply on particular incidents, I became aware of the part of me that enabled me to respond. I then realized how much in control and how strong I could be in times of crisis. I also realized that if I could become strong, so can anyone else.

So, once a person has consciously or instinctively decided on their response and resolved to start to implement it, they enter the sixth phase.

Phase VI. Response
You do it - and you get through it. *You survive.* You will still experience fear, but you can stay focused on your tactics and actions. You will do everything and anything it takes to survive.

Dr. Solomon described his model as a method to inoculate yourself against fear. The key to it is being prepared in advance of trouble, so you can act appropriately when danger strikes.

This model perfectly describes what it is like to 'walk into' a situation where there is a suggestion of a warning that something bad could happen. In my opinion, this model should be etched in the mind of every person whose occupation involves a threat to life.

But what about preparing yourself for something that is not even on the radar yet? What about someone wanting to get over a phobia, or at least bring it under control?

I have adapted it to identify five steps that, with deeper understanding, describe what people can do to control any fear they have.

FEAR CONTROL PROCESS

All of us experience fear, but when we confront and acknowledge it, we can turn it into courage.

— Desmond Tutu

I mentioned before that Dr. Solomon's model was a great awakening for me. I had been through the process he describes many times, and to see it laid out in black and white was a great relief. It made me realize that I was normal and that those who criticized my preoccupation with operational risks were not facing the reality of a dangerous occupation.

As real and accurate as Dr. Solomon's model is, I learned from experience to start the process much earlier than his model describes. I wanted to get myself to the "oh oh" phase well in advance of anything happening and preparing myself for the "oh shit" phase long before the shit hit the fan, so to speak.

Practically everything I experience in life is a lesson for me, and I try to identify the obscure meanings behind every event, occurrence, and setback. It is an ongoing quest to get me a head-start on the next problem that comes down the pike. Another model or way of looking at controlling fear was not going to hurt.

I realized that five factors needed to be overcome, which are common to every situation that I knew caused me fear. Those factors are:

1. Confusion
2. Aversion
3. Confrontation
4. Crisis
5. Consequences

From the earliest days in the police force, my main worry was dealing with violent people. I wanted to be one of the people capable of standing up to them and defeating them.

My starting point was to learn as much as I could about the theory of human anger and aggression. Couple with the experience I was accumulating, I identified the types of violence I could be called to deal with and the skills I needed to deal with them. The more I learned, and the more I practiced, the more confident I became.

Put simply, I needed to build up these five pillars:
1. Knowledge
2. Skills
3. Courage
4. Action
5. Survival

Over the years, I became aware that I was using a regular pattern to achieve those five goals. It was adaptable to any type of adversity.

After I left the police force and got into my own business, I faced a whole new range of unknown situations that created varying degrees of fear. Merely leaving the security of the police force to start my own business is but one example.

As every new challenge appeared, I relied on the only way I knew about how to cope with fear and uncertainty. This is my way of dealing with every challenge that comes my way:
1. Learning
2. Accepting
3. Preparing
4. Responding
5. Recovering

When I map the process, it works like this - I address a fear-factor using a control measure to give me the desired outcome.

Factor	Control	Outcome
Confusion	Learn	Knowledge
Aversion	Accept	Skills
Confrontation	Prepare	Courage
Crisis	Respond	Action
Consequences	Recover	Survive

These are some of the ways that this process has helped me:
- Motivated my curiosity about life's adversities and how to overcome them so I can live my life to its full potential.

- Problem solving
- Learning to fight the fear of something by understanding it and gradually exposing myself to it in a safe environment.
- Learning to recognize my negative thoughts, challenge them, and think of winning ways to respond to a situation.
- Develop a single-minded focus on the reality of the present moment.
- Acknowledging and accepting my thoughts, feelings, and physical sensations of my body as being natural and helpful.
- Learning the knowledge, strategies, skills, tactics, techniques, and variations of each to combat various challenging situations.
- Accept my vulnerabilities and develop realistic physical and mental defense systems.
- I learned how to work through chaos and deal with those around me who panic and cannot think for themselves.
- The ability to rapidly prioritize action against practical, moral, and legal obligations.
- Ability to rationalize outcomes and consequences and release tension and stress.

Here are some additional tips on what you can use in the process to control fear.

- Develop your mental skills, along with your physical skills. One is no value without the other period.
- Practice what you need to apply in a real-life situation. Keep it simple and realistic according to your capability to execute.
- Set yourself tasks to practice that are specific and measurable.
- Set tasks that are difficult but realistic. Train to race, do not race to train.
- Set short-term, intermediate, and long-term goals. Nothing worthwhile comes easy.
- Think positive (like "better than last time") as opposed to negative (like "still not as good as I want to be"). Step by step to success.
- Remain flexible to adjust your realistic expectations as needed. Physical capability decreases over time.
- Emphasize performance over outcome. Your best is good enough – winning is a bonus.

People tend to want to have the problem in their face before they start to react to it. It is like looking into a rail tunnel, not realizing that the light you see is a train coming. Then suddenly it appears as if you never knew it was a train coming.

Armed with the fear-fighting tools, fear becomes manageable and a productive stimulus that can create opportunity. But if you don't possess and deploy these tools, the fear you feel is probably well-founded and actually giving you good advice.

The only way to make sure your fear is a motivator and not an immobilizer is through performance.

To prepare for the future:

- Understand the environment you are going to operate in.
- Learn the skills, tactics, and techniques you need.
- Get the training you need and keep up your skills.
- Understand the psychological and physical effects of fear in that environment.
- Acknowledge the reality of what can happen now.
- Reinforce your will to succeed and survive.
- Remember past successes in similar circumstances.
- Utilize fear to become strong.
- Mentally rehearse scenarios and what you will do to deal with them.

CONCLUSION

Learning to handle fear and overcome it so you can make wise decisions is critical to avoiding anxiety and fully living your life.

The way I see it, our first instinct is to avoid anything that we perceive to be dangerous. Although this instinct evolved to protect us, it limits our personal growth and sense of achievement if we are not realistic.

Irrational and unresolved fear keeps us from getting what we want and becoming who we honestly deep down want to be.

If allowed to, fear can grow deep roots. Roots that become so embedded that, like a plant, we feed them with negative thoughts. Once we convince ourselves that fear is valid and real, it takes a special kind of 'psychological weedkiller' to remove it.

We need 'weedkillers' to get rid of those roots to make our world more comfortable and stable. These are good fear weedkillers:

- Expect the unexpected.
- Make the unfamiliar familiar.
- Make the unknown known.
- Make the uncomfortable comfortable.
- Believe the unbelievable.

Many people are suffering who live or work in environments that give them fear. They are stressed, sad, and do not know what to do. The suffering will be made worse for those people who deny it, hide from it, or try to escape from it in an unhealthy way.

It is essential to know that it takes a lot of energy to deny or hide from fear. The longer you deny fear, the more you try to escape it or cover it up. You will suffer more until the stress becomes unbearable and causes you to break down.

Many people suffer debilitating stress from living with unresolved fear. Many do not realize that PTSD is largely the result of unresolved fear arising from one or more critical incidents. They try to ignore the suffering they feel.

Many try to cover it by turning to alcohol, sex, drugs, or other stimulant abuse types. If you do that, you will feel more suffering than ever. Think skid row.

When we feel fear, when we know that something makes us afraid, when we know something we fear could happen to us, we should do something about it. We should harmonize with our fears, to use them for encouragement and building our strength.

We could make fun out of it. For example, facing fears through learning, training, sport, or other safe experiences can be enjoyable. By learning all we can about what we are afraid of, we can live comfortably with it.

If we swim against the flow of water, we need to use a lot of power. But if we just follow the flow or at least swim across it, we feel more comfortable. It is the same as suffering from fear. The suffering will not stay with us so long if we understand our fear, confront it, and use its power to propel us forward into action.

Some words of caution. Be careful who you chose to talk to about your fear, especially if you are dealing with critical incident stress.

We should not take the story of our experience and suffering to just anyone. When people listen to our experience and suffering, they probably will not understand unless they have experienced the same thing. They probably cannot help with anything anyway.

Importantly, we can suffer more when we talk about our suffering to someone who does not understand what we have experienced. People who do not understand can say stupid things that can cause us to become angry and resentful.

If you want to tell your story, tell it to someone who has experienced the same thing and can help you in some beneficial way. These are people who listen to us with true understanding.

Do not blame yourself for anything. When they are unhappy and stressed, many people blame themselves when they are suffering because they think they are at fault. They think of their weaknesses and mistakes and believe they deserve the suffering. If we are blaming ourselves, who else will understand us? Who can help us if we cannot help ourselves first?

So, it is important to cheer and encourage ourselves when we are suffering from fear and stress. The more we do that for ourselves, the more we support ourselves. The way it works is to encourage ourselves as much as possible. Tell ourselves that we have something good to be proud of. We have done things to be proud of. We have done things that many others could never do. We, you, are warriors.

Of course, it can be difficult for some people to find the good things in their lives when they are suffering. We need to find all our good things and write them down if necessary (count our blessings) to remind ourselves.

Do not overthink things. The top of everyone's list should be that they are alive. Everything after that is a bonus.

Control your fears and be at peace within yourselves, for blessed are the peacemakers.

THE PEACEMAKER

The author's second book is about dealing with cyber-bullying.

Widely accused by conspiracy theorists of being the shooter at the Port Arthur Massacre, the author tells of his involvement in the police operation and reveals the threats and abuse he has continued to receive for more than 15 years.

Actual messages and his replies are revealed in the book and he uses these to explain a systematic method to combat cyber-bullies and make them leave you alone.

www.ingramcontent.com/pod-product-compliance
Lightning Source LLC
Chambersburg PA
CBHW060501280326
41933CB00014B/2816